THE GREAT AWAKENING

Volume XIV

Temple Teachings from the
Higher Realms

Sister Thedra

Copyright © 2021 by Halls of Light, LLC

All rights reserved. This book or any portion thereof may not be reproduced or used in any manner whatsoever without the express written permission of the publisher except for the use of brief quotations in a book review.

ISBN: 978-1-7366487-7-3

To the Reader

This book is only a portion of the teachings and prophecies that have been given by Sananda, Sanat Kumara, and others of the higher realms, and Recorded by Sister Thedra.

Contents

PORTIONS OF THE SIBORS 1

EXCERPTS FROM THE SIBORS INSTRUCTIONS 23

THE SEAL 137

TO THE ONES IN HIGH PLACES 153

MOTHER SARA 229

Mission Statement 239

Sananda's Appearance 240

Authority to Use the Name Sananda 241

About the Late Sister Thedra 243

Esu Jesus Sananda

This reproduction is from an actual photograph taken on June 1st, 1961, in Chichen Itza, Yucatan, by one of thirty archaeologists working in the area at the time. Sananda appeared in visible, tangible body and permitted His photograph to be taken.

PORTIONS OF THE SIBORS

Stephani Speaking

I have spoken unto them that they may turn unto Me before it comes upon them--that great and terrible day--when a great wind shall blow from pole to pole---which shall burn all which it touches. And it shall sweep the earth as NO-THING seen by man!

And it shall be the day which the ancients have spoken of-- which has not been remembered by the ones which have gone from one embodiment to another with the mind blanked---

No memory of their past experience---

No memory of Me-----

And no LIGHT within them--they are the sad ones.

I am in the mood to bring them home---yet I wait upon them-- that they may come of their own accord.

My face I shall turn from them which spit upon thee My child---for I say I shall lift thee up in the time of their sleep--and they shall know it not!

I say unto thee I shall lift thee up -- I shall raise thee up in the time of their sleep---and they shall sleep on!

And they shall be as the traitors---I say: "there are none so sad as them which betray themself" - so be it and Selah.

I command thee --- GIVE THIS UNTO THEM IN MY NAME.

And I shall make of thee a prophet in thy own right.

So be it My Word has gone out--and It shall return unto Me in this day -- so be it I am the Father which has given unto thee being.

Amen and SELAH.

Blest are they which come together in My name - and for the purpose of learning of Me.

I Am thy Father which has given unto thee being.

I Am that which ye are - and I Am now revealing Myself unto thee for the purpose of bringing thee out of bondage - for the purpose of bringing thee home.

I Am come into the world of flesh made manifest - that which I have created may know Me - and may know that I now endow unto them all that I Am. And I say unto them which I have given being - that I Am the Cause of thy being --

And I Am He which has created all that is created - I create the creators --

I give unto My own the power and the authority to create like unto Me - I give unto them that which I Am - and I Am not divided --

I Am Whole - I Am within all that which I have created.

And they which expound their theories about Me are as fools indeed for they know Me not!

I Am come unto thee in tangible proof that I Am.

And where I Am there ye shall be also.

I have sent My Son unto thee - and ye have received Him in My Name - and as ye have received Him so shall ye receive Me -- and as ye receive Me so shall ye receive of Me thy GODHOOD - and for this have ye waited.

I Am glad this day is come for I have waited long for thy return unto Me.

I say the day has come when many from the sleepers realm shall be lifted up from among them - and they which sleep shall sleep on unknowingly.

For they shall go into their new place of abode unaware of Me and unprepared for their next part.

Now let it be said again: "There is none so sad as the one which betrays himself". He is the fool.

I say it is the foolish one which says he is wise - for he which is wise gives unto Me credit - for he is aware of Me in all things - he takes no credit unto himself - for I Am He which IS - has been - and ever shall be. So be it and Selah.

I Am the gate through which he passes --

I Am he which passes --

I Am the Alpha and the Omega -

I Am --

I shall be in the beginning -

I was --

In the end I shall be.

I say that he which thinks himself to be - shall pass away - shall become NO-THING - and shall be no more.

I Am everlasting -unto everlasting.

I come not - Neither do I go -

I AM.

And I say unto thee ye shall come to know Me to be thyself --

And I AM GLAD - for this do I reveal Myself unto thee --

I AM glad this day is come when I may open My mouth - and they shall hear My words - for I shall cause My words to be put into thy mouth - And I shall cause them to hear and to comprehend them.

I am not of a mind to sacrifice My own - for I have watched thee diligently search for Me in all thy ways - and for this do I reveal Myself unto thee.

I Am with thee - and each within the place wherein My words are being recorded shall have proof of Me.

I have spoken and My words SHALL return unto Me in this day. So be it and Selah.

I AM thy Father, Solen.

Spoken to a group of Initiates through Sister Thedra of The Emerald Cross.

Father-Mother God:

I come to this Thy Altar which Thou hast set up - with no thought but to serve Thee here where Thou hast directed me to serve - that THY WILL may be done in us - through us - by us and for us - So be it unto THEE, all the Power, and the Glory forever, Amen. Thedra.

Wherein have I said that I shall make of thee a prophet in thy own right?

I say it is now come when ye shall be given the authority and the power to say unto them that which I shall give unto thee to say - for ye shall go out into the world of them and ye shall speak the words which I shall give unto thee to say.

And thy tongue shall be loosed - and thy hands shall be untied - and ye shall be as My feet made manifest upon the Earth.

For it is near the time when great sorrow shall come upon them - And they shall call out for deliverance.

And I have said that I am a merciful God - and I too have said I shall send one unto them which shall be qualified to lift them up --

And too I have said - that they which turn their face from Me - and which do set their hand against My prophets shall surely be cast out. For I have given unto them free will - and if they choose to return unto

Me I shall receive them - and I shall give unto them their inheritance in full - So be it and Selah.

Now give this unto them - and when they reject it, give unto them no more.

And I say that they which do reject it shall be as one which has betrayed himself - and sad shall he be for he shall be caught up short of his course.

And he shall be as one cast into darkness and despair.

I say I have given them free will - and I shall not trespass upon it - So be it and Selah.

I Am now speaking unto thee that they which have not asked of Me might receive these My words.

And too have I not said that ALL I have is thine?

And have I not said that as they prepare themself so shall they receive - So be it and Selah.

Now have "They" not set their hand unto thy mouth?

Have "They" not sealed thy lips?

And now I say that they which have sealed thy lips are cut off from Me.

And yet I AM not cut off from them -- for I AM THEY - yet I am not as yet revealed unto them - for they close Me out --

I am in the place wherein I AM

And I AM He which knows all things --

Yet they which do close Me out make of Me a thing separate - and apart.

I AM not divided - I AM WHOLE -

I AM the ALPHA and the OMEGA

I AM thyself -

And unto them which choose to return unto Me I shall give him the cup of LIVING WATER --

I say I shall send one of My emissaries unto him and he shall give unto him water which he knows not of --

For within My hand I hold such substance as he is filled.

Ye have been given much which ye have recorded for them - and they as yet have not been given the comprehension which is of Me - they understand it not! I see them as ones which sit bowed down in the world of men - they run hither and fro - knowing not from whence they came - neither do they know whither they goest - Sad is the lot.

I am about to cast them out -

Yet I have said that it is the law that they be warned - that they choose this day which way they go --

So be it I stand ready to receive them --

Yet they have to receive My prophets - My Sons - and my emissaries in My Name.

Yet I say unto them it is now come upon the sad Earth - that one shall rise up - and he shall call himself God --

He shall do all manner of miracles --

He shall call them just --

He shall put the whore on the goat.

He shall bless them with words of honey --

He shall pilfer their pockets --

He shall call them fools --

He shall confuse them.

He shall be as the DRAGON ensouled in flesh.

He shall be the dark one - and LIGHT shall be no part of him

Yet I say unto thee my child Thedra, that they shall bow down unto him. they shall kiss the ground on which he walks --

He shall carry within his hand a staff of gold - set with pearls and rubies --

He shall sit upon an altar which he has set up -

And he shall call for the sacrifice of human blood --

And he shall be as demon possessed --

I say he is the daemon --

I say he is the DRAGON cast down.

Now I shall call this one by name - and ye shall remember it.

For I say as yet he has not revealed himself.

Yet he shall - and I am not so minded to deliver up My own - them which choose to return unto Me.

I shall allow them their way - the ones which choose to follow him the Dragon.

Yet I shall deliver up them which choose to return unto Me. Now I have said that any one whichever - and wherever they be which do spit upon My words - or set hand unto My prophet shall be cut down.

I have spoken - and I shall manifest Myself in ways they know not of.

Such is My Nature - and such is My Name -

I AM HE which has created ALL that is created WELL - created GOOD.

I AM --

And I shall always Be - So be it and Selah

Whore - the one which creates imperfectly

The goat - the intellectual mind.

Recorded by Sister Thedra

Father-Mother God: I Thedra come unto this Thy Altar that you give unto us the story which has begun -

We accept Thy Emissaries, Servants or Sons as Thou see fit. Thank You - Unto Thee all the Glory. So be it Amen.

Sarah, Mother of Abraham - Speaking unto thee my child - I am One which has waited this hour for much has been said about this subject - the fall of man - Now let it be said that when there was but little light upon the Earth not one which dwelt there upon was sufficient unto himself -

They walked upon the four feet and they had not yet walked upon the two - For it was given unto them to be as beasts which had been placed upon Earth by the one which was cast down - I say that the beast was the outcome of the dragon - For the Father Mother God - does not create like unto the whore -

For it is given unto Us to be perfect and anything unlike perfection is of the dragon - I say that the dragon had the right to call himself God for he knew all things - He was of the Father born - He had received his inheritance in full - Yet he had the audacity to call himself father of all that is and was ---

He used the law for his end and he gave no heed unto the warning of the Father for it was brought before the Great Council that which was being done - And when he which is called Lucifer was given an ultimatum he called together his followers and he said unto them- Ye have seen my work have I not created these things - have I not cast into the deep these creatures which shall devour their flesh - have I not given unto these things life and have I not been with thee these days - wherein have ye aught against me - if ye follow me I shall make of thee great and wondrous beings ---

I shall give unto thee the greatest and shining star within the firmament and when they gazed upon his handiwork they fell down and did worship him - I say unto thee great was and is their sorrow---

For unto this day do they pay the price - I am weary for them for I see them as ones bound hand and foot and they cry out for deliverance-

Yet they ask not for light - for he has held them bound lo the eons of time I care not to say how long - Pray for them that they may turn homeward and we shall receive them with a joyous heart - Wait for another part - This is not done -

I am thy Mother Sarah

Father-Mother God - What would You have of me this day? Thedra

Blest art thou my child - I am now prepared to continue the discourse of the fall of Lucifer - So shall ye begin where we left off - I am thy Mother Sarah - Was it not said that there was war in heaven? And was it not so? For it was given unto one which was as a Son of God to betray himself For he had the power invested within him of God the Father to create even worlds - yea to create and to populate them - And he has within his power even to this day to create them.

Yet I say unto thee my daughter Thedra that when he gave unto himself and when he took unto himself the glory he became as one puffed up - As one rebellious - And he gathered about him the ones which were of like mind and they gave unto him great glory and they were fascinated by his words - And by his miracles - And he gave unto them words of praise and appointed unto them grand places and stations and called them by great sounding names and brought royal raiment and placed it upon them with great high courts attending –

He brought from out the firmament flaming chariots wherein were legions which came from out thy own solar system - He gave unto them the corner stone for the voice which would sound throughout the universe - I say he gave unto them the instrument which would serve him and that instrument is known throughout the solar system for it is the voice of the one known as Lucifer - - -

I say that upon the altar of Lucifer stands one which has within him the power to turn nation against nation - Brother against brother - I say that the altar upon which he sits is the corner stone which was laid at the beginning of his reign - He has laid the plan and likewise has he laid the corner stone -

Such is my love and wisdom I can see them bound in darkness crying out as little children frightened of the dark - I am within the place wherein I am prepared to receive them when they are prepared to be brought home - Be as one which has the will to return unto me - And I shall be as one prepared to receive thee in love mercy and wisdom -

When the war of the heavens was but begun there was one which ye know as Michael which was and is the first Son of God the Father He has the first place He has been called Michael the First and there are none other Michael The First - Yet there are other Michaels - Ye know Him too as Prince Michael - for He is indeed a Prince in His own right for from the beginning has He been Prince -

I say He is indeed a Prince - for am I not the Mother of Him - Am I not Queen of Queens - Have I not sat on the throne of Thrones? Have I not been all the things a queen should be - Have I not given life unto my sons - My own precious life that they may become Gods within their own right? Have I not brought them into manifestation for the purpose of glorifying the Father upon the Earth that they might fulfill that plan - for which they were given being -

Now when the war was but begun - Michael was the One which came forth as the Defender of Truth and Justice - He it was which gave unto Lucifer the ultimatum which banished him into the world of darkness - Even then when the Earth was in another part of the firmament and before her axis was changed - was she a dark planet.

I say she was and is a dark planet - little light goes out from her - And for this reason has certain of My children volunteered to take upon themself physical bodies - of earthly substance that the planet Earth might be held within her orbit for the time when she might come into the fullness of her inheritance - So be it and Selah - Now when certain ones which come into the planet Earth volunteers to do so they are not denied - And with great difficulty do they lower their light that they may walk in thy midst -

And upon their head is a crown not seen by man yet We see it and We send one with them that they may have a companion - And that they may be sustained for their stay within the Earth - Now when this was accomplished that Lucifer was cast out of heaven and to the dark planet Earth he set about to all manner of experiments - He used the sea for his playground –

He created the porpoise - He created the whale and he gave life to the walrus and the seal - Even unto the mammoth turtle which carries more than his weight upon his back - for this was but the experiments of one Lucifer which has not as yet finished his hand work - I say unto thee my child unto this day does he make of mortal a plaything - I say he uses life for his own gratification of the sense he satisfies his own longing by roguish means - He gives no thought of his Godhood which was endowed unto him - And he has been as one imprisoned upon and within the Earth for a long period of time –

Yet I say he shall be removed forever and the Earth shall be freed from all pollution - all memory of him. So be it he shall be bound in yet another place of darkness and he shall take with him his legions which choose to follow him - So be it that the Earth shall have a new berth and a new birth - For she too shall be born again -

She shall go through the baptism of fire and she shall be purified unto the last atom - I say she shall be purified unto the last atom - Now go into the place wherein ye shall find one which shall be glad to find a place for these words and prepare them for Him and He shall give them unto the ones which are seeking light and they shall be quickened and I shall reveal unto them many things and they shall be glad for I have caused these words to be written for a purpose - I have in mind a plan and I am not given unto foolishness - So be it I have commanded thee and ye shall obey in love and wisdom -

I shall lead thee and ye shall be glad - I am thy Mother Sarah -

Recorded by Sister Thedra

Through Sister Thedra of the Emerald Cross

The following is an excerpt from the message concerning the preparation for our first meeting in the Temple of Sananda- Sanat Kumara.

Sanat Kumara speaking -

Say unto them - They shall arise at the dawn each day and they shall have themselves dressed and presented at the altar at the time of sunrise and ye shall sit with thy face to the east and ye shall seat thy ---- at thy right hand and ye shall give unto him thy right hand and he shall give unto thee his left and ye shall stand as one - whereupon ye shall sit shall be a seat which is large enough for the two -

For ye shall be as one - And then when ye have seated thyself one shall prepare for thee a cup of fresh water which shall be handed unto thee - Ye shall sup from it and pass it unto thy ---- and he shall drink what is within the cup - For I say unto thee this is but the beginning ---

When ye have learned this part I shall groom thee for the greater part and ye shall follow this part with thy whole heart until it is perfected and then ye shall have a new part added unto that which I am now giving unto thee - So be it that it shall be different in form - yet it shall be part of this the first -

I say ye shall be as ones which have thy heart in this part - For I say this part shall be held sacred and ye shall not desecrate it - I say woe unto the one which treats it lightly for he shall be as a traitor unto himself - So be it and Selah -

* * *

Later - Same Day - Concerning Naming of Temple

Sanat Kumara speaking -

I say unto thee which sit at thy council table that I am the director of this certain activity and within the plan are many activities, for it is the day of action - and action there shall be and now - Ye which have gathered thyself at this council table shall be informed that there are many such councils - and many which seeks the light ---

And with the one which has been sent unto this head of this activity which is the Priestess of Sananda and which is ordained of God the Father, shall he which is sent be coordinator and co-regent of this temple within this part of this activity.

I say that there are many such activities, but this one shall be called the "Center of Sananda and Sanat Kumara", for within this center shall we as co-workers within the realms of light, direct this center and bring it into its proper focus - Such is our part at this time. I shall speak unto thee later - S.K.

Sanat Kumara, speaking -

Now my sister of the Emerald Cross - Ye have assembled within this place for the purpose of learning of me and ye shall be true unto thyself and say unto these within this temple that they shall abide by the law which shall be set down - And for this shall ye be prepared - For it is now come when ye shall be given the law which was spoken of in the Priory which was aborted - I say that they which were called from the dragons den did abort the first effort to which I say not a plan goes astray - Only the sheep-

Now I say unto thee ye shall say unto them in my name that when it is come that they are prepared to enter into my place of abode they shall be glad - So be it and Selah -

Now will it so that they keep their peace and hold their tongue - for it is now come when they shall learn the meaning of silence - I say not one word of aught shall escape thy lips of thy brothers short comings - And not one word of mockery - For it is a pitfall - For within this temple shall be the great and the near great -

And too I say none are greater - None the smallest for there shall be equality and justice in all things - Yet I say some shall go out before thee to prepare the way for thee and yet ye shall follow after them which goes before thee - I say they are great because and for the reason that one shall go out before thee that ye may receive thy inheritance even as that one has received - So be it and Selah -

Now wherein is it said there are none so foolish as the one which thinks himself wise - So be it a truth indeed - I am thy Sibor and I am thy brother - So be it and Selah -

I am - Sanat Kumara

Sanat Kumara speaking -

Ye have gathered thyself to gather within this temple as a living example of that which shall be come - I say unto thee ye shall be as the hands and feet of God the Father and ye shall walk in the way set before thee.

I am the Comanche within this temple for God the Father has asked that I set up this temple - for it is now time that this be accomplished - And ye shall play a part within the building of a temple not builded with hands within this place - for that temple shall first be built within the ether and lowered into the earthy vibration -

One morning they shall awaken and find to their amazement the temple not built with hands shining upon the mountain and then they shall wonder and they shall ponder long upon it and too - They shall be more confounded when they cannot draw neigh unto it - For there shall be a mighty barrier about and none shall penetrate its field without the proper preparation -

Now for the second time ye have come - I say it is forgivable when ye are not so instructed as to the ways of the temple procedure - Yet ye are instructed - It is the first law to obey - For there are none so foolish as to disobey - He betrays himself - This is the law which we, thy Sibors live by - And for this do we have our inheritance -

I am now prepared to lay my hand upon thee and to bless thee as I have been blest - Yet I cannot come until ye have prepared thyself to receive me and ye first have to be of a mind to prepare thyself and to give of thyself - And I say unto thee - first things first -

And then when ye have finished the first - second step shall be taken Now I say unto the one which has broken a very strict ---- that he has been a one which has been bound by the dark one - He has been found ---- napping while he-the dark one has not slept - He does not sleep. He is not even willing to give unto his followers an hour of rest - He pushes them -

He gives them no peace! He grows fat on their labor - He gives unto them nothing but torment - He gives not even mercy - He gives no relief He has no lasting reward - He gives no freedom - He has only lasting and intolerant punishment - for them which follow him - Yet I say he holds them fast!

I say I stand before thee as one which the Father has sent unto thee/ I plead with thee - Be ye alert - Be ye filled with love of light - Be ye as one prepared to receive me and of me - For I come that ye may be loosed from all bondage -

I say I am come to unbind thee - I am now prepared to unbind thee and I would give unto thee a few laws which shall profit thee --

First I shall give unto thee: There are none so foolish as the one which thinks himself wise - And none so foolish as the one which betrays himself or his trust -

Second - There are none great - None small -

Third - There are no servants within this temple - There are only the sibets which are the initiates on the path - None have received their Godhood -

I say ye are sibets and I say ye shall be a living example of a sibet of the initiate with the consideration and respect one for the other - Ye shall be as ones mindful of that which ye represent - That which is given unto thee to do - for as ye for one moment lose sight of thy goal thy responsibility - thy part as a sibet - at that moment - the dark forces have gained entrance into thy field and ye have lost ground - And for this has he, Lucifer won a point -

I have commanded thee be ye alert and as yet ye have not comprehended what I am saying -

I shall give unto thee of myself that ye may have comprehension - yet I say I have set up this altar in the name of the Father Son and Holy Ghost - So be it Amen - and when it is come that one does not begin his day with the first p. therein is the first thing ye shall remember - And the initiate which cannot or will not make this his motto is at once by his own self cut off -

We do not cut him off - I say when ye have been given a commandment once - it does not become obsolete - It remains as valid and shall not become obsolete or invalid - for there are no mistakes in the law - which is given within the temple - and there are no foolish sayings -

Now were it not so dark within the world of men we should not be at this altar for there are none which has been prepared for the inner temple wherein I am the Master of Initiation - I am the Most Worthy Grand Master - and I am he which gives thee thy passport into the inner temple where in the Father abides -

I give unto thee passport into all the secret places within the earth -

I give unto thee thy cloak not made with hands - I give unto thee thy orb and thy scepter - I am the Master of Ceremony - I am the Comanche -

Will ye not be mindful of thy ways? Will ye not be as ones alert - And ask of thyself many things and ye shall not excuse thy short sightedness - nor shall ye shift the blame - I say ye shall not blame another for thy short comings! Ye stand fully responsible for thy actions and the result thereof - Ye shall not criticize another - nor point a finger at another -

Ye shall not be judge of the actions of another - Ye shall be unto thy brother tolerant - Yet ye shall not join with him in his folly -

Ye shall be a thing unto thyself - Ye shall dare to be different from him - Ye shall give unto him no word of scorn or <u>nothing</u> which he shall <u>trip over</u> which would confuse him for he too seeks the light in dark places -

Ye shall watch thy tongue for it is a tricky thing! And a subtle weapon!

Ye shall have within thy heart love for all things which are created good! Ye shall be as ones prepared for thy own Godhood -

Ye shall be as ones which has upon thy head a crown and ye shall walk in a way which it tilts not. Now when ye have been prepared I shall give unto thee the power to command the elements - and to create like unto the Father - for He has given unto me this part as my inheritance - So be it His will that I shall prepare thee and for this have I been prepared -

Now I would command thee - Go from this altar in silence and give unto thyself nothing to eat this day and to be mindful of this thy part - And when ye have been so prepared I shall give unto thee a portion which shall be unto thee much strength -

I am Sanat Kumara -

Sister Thedra of the Emerald Cross

EXCERPTS FROM THE SIBORS INSTRUCTIONS

"I say unto thee: Ye shall forgive thyself and turn from thy own guilt - and ye shall be as one forgiven - Ye shall ask no man forgiveness for <u>thy guilt</u> - yet if ye have given another pain <u>wontonly</u> or deliberately, ye shall hasten to correct it for it is the better part of wisdom.

So be it and Selah - Philus."

Sanat Kumara speaking -

Beloved children which has gathered thyself to gather at this altar which God the Father has set up - Say I unto thee ye shall be as ones on which I shall place great responsibility - And I say unto thee - Ye shall prepare thyself for the part which I shall give unto thee - Ye shall prove thyself worthy of the great responsibility - for it is now come when great changes shall come about upon the earth and among her people -

I say that the hierarchy has commanded that each and every one be prepared for their new places - their new parts - for many shall go. into their new places without any preparation and therein is great pity for there are the sleepers which have slept for centuries without any knowledge of that which go on around about them - Now when they go into their new place of abode fully aware of their condition -

And when they are of a mind to learn - they pass from darkness into light with no pain - no sorrow - no longing - And they do not taste of death - for there is a plan which has been prepared for you which are of a mind to learn and - Ye shall be given the fullness within this temple when ye are prepared - For I say that within this temple which shall be called the Temple of Sananda -Sanat Kumara - one shall stand and declare for thee thy freedom - for I shall stand within the place wherein ye are and I shall give unto thee - which prepare thyself the cup of life I shall personally give unto thee as I have received of God the Father - So be it my word unto thee -

Now I say unto thee: ye have come unto this place of thy own free will and ye are of a mind to learn - Yet I say beware of the pitfalls for they are subtle - And many - I say be ye alert and be ye mindful of us thy Sibors - Be ye respectful one for the other - Be ye responsible for thy own actions - Give not unto thy brother a tack for his shoe - Be ye as a lamp unto his feet -

Go in peace - Walk in the Light of the Christ - Remember whence thy blessings. -

I am Sanat Kumara -

Sister Thedra of the Emerald Cross

Quote from The Preparation of the Initiate

"When one of the children of the earth is liberated from bondage- from the wheel of re-birth - and has found his eternal freedom there is great rejoicing throughout the cosmos - and great is the preparation for this day when many shall be delivered out -

So be it and Selah" Philus

Sanat Kumara speaking -

I say unto thee which have assembled within this temple which the Father has caused to be brought forth - that one among thee shall be as my hand made manifest - and one shall be my mouth - And one shall be as the hand of God the Father - for it is now come when great and trying times shall come upon thee and ye shall be as ones prepared for them -

I say that this is the better part of wisdom to prepare thyself first - Ye have been prepared for this part yet ye have not begun thy work - for great things are in store for thee and great shall be the revelation for them which are prepared for such -

I say great are the revelations which shall be revealed unto the just and the worthy - For this have we waited -

I am now prepared to give unto thee that which I have kept for thee. And when ye have brot into focus the great and divine plan - and put aside thy trivial things and thy puny ways - thy childishness and given unto this plan of thyself - and thy strength with thy whole heart I shall give unto thee a greater part - So be it in the name of the Father Son and Holy Ghost - Amen and Selah -

I am the Comanche within these chambers and I shall watch thee and thy reaction one unto the other - And I shall be as one prepared for any occasion any situation -

Now let it be said none are indispensable - I say none are indispensable - And not a plan goes astray - Yet I say my sheep are of a mind to wander afar - It is given unto them to bolt and to get lost - I am going to give unto thee a parable which shall profit thee --

When a lamb goes into the fold - he knows not his origin and he knows not his destination for he is but an animal without memory and when the one bound has his memory blanked from him he is little above the animal - yet the shepherd which we thy Sibors are have the power and the authority to restore it unto thee - Such is our inheritance -

I shall give unto thee as ye are capable of receiving -

So be it in the name of the Father Son and Holy Ghost - Amen - Selah

I am Sanat Kumara -

Go in Peace

Sheloheim Adomni -

Sister Thedra of the Emerald Cross

Sananda speaking:

Ye shall hear this, my part and ye shall be unto thyself true and remember it and ye shall hold it within thy heart and abide by it - I give unto thee one commandment this day - And ye shall be as one which has my hand upon thee - Give unto them this commandment for this day --

"Let no word defile thy lips."

Sananda

Sanat Kumara speaking -

I have given unto this day one commandment - "Let no word defile thy lips." Let only peace be within thee - Let only Love reign within this temple - I say Love is the cure for ALL thy woes - All thy longings. Love cureth All disease regardless of appearance -

Be unto thyself True and give unto no man the bitter cup -

I am the Most Worthy Grand Master within this temple which has been long coming forth -

Yet it is not as yet perfected and I say that there shall be trying days ahead and many pitfalls - Yet I say ye shall stand as the rock upon which I shall build a great and wondrous temple - So be it in the name of the Father Son and Holy Ghost - Amen -

Ye shall have no gods before thee - Ye shall be as one which has a will to return unto the Father which has given unto thee being - Ye shall begin thy day with the words "Oh Father-Mother God I am one with thee - I have come unto this thy altar for the purpose of learning thy will and I bring myself as a living sacrifice - Accept my offering I ask in thy name and thru thy grace I shall return unto thee - I am he which thou has blest with life and I am glad".

Be ye at peace and poise this day and ye shall receive of the Father Son and Holy Ghost - Amen and Selah -

I am Sanat Kumara -

Sister Thedra of the Emerald Cross

Osiris speaking -

Beloved of my being -

Be ye blest of me and by me - I am come that ye may be blest - I am now within the place wherein I am prepared for the part which I shall now give unto thee - And I say unto thee: ye have prepared thyself for this part which shall be given unto thee -

Now when it was given unto thee to be sent out from thy homeland into the south ye knew not that ye should return unto thy homeland - Then when ye returned unto thy homeland ye knew not that ye would return unto the land to the south - Now I say unto thee ye shall go into the land of the Andes and ye shall therein find one which has upon his head a crown not made with hands - and I say unto thee ye shall walk among them as one of them -

Ye shall be unto them sister - Ye shall be unto them as one of them I say ye shall return unto them which are known as the Royal Assembly Ye shall go into the place where none other has been brought - For this have ye been prepared -

Now I say unto thee ye shall go out from the place wherein ye are as one prepared - Ye shall need no passport nor shall ye carry any portfolio - I say ye shall be as one free from the law of gravity and ye shall be free of all bondage -

I say unto thee ye shall go out with one which has been sent unto thee - I say ye have been brot together for the purpose of bringing about thy ascension - I say ye shall ascend together I say ye have been brot together that this may be accomplished -

Now I say unto thee which has been given this great privilege that it is by the GRACE of one which we know as our beloved Sanat Kumara and our beloved Lord and Master Sananda which is the way shower that this new dispensation has been brought into focus -

I say that He Sananda, is The Wayshower - I say ye have chosen to follow Him - and I am glad - I say unto thee blest are they which do follow Him for they shall not taste of death - Such is my word unto thee And by His GRACE shall ye overcome the flesh - And with my being I bless thee and I shall sustain thee and I shall give unto thee as ye are prepared to receive - Such is my part -

Now ye shall go into the temple which has been established within the place wherein ye are and ye shall give unto them this word - And ye shall be as one in authority when ye say that which I have given unto thee to say - for I am not a fool - Nor do I betray myself - for I am of the Father sent - And He has given unto me my inheritance in full - So be it and Selah -

Now I say unto thee ye shall stand before the altar of the Most High Living God and receive of Him thy inheritance in full - And ye shall go out as one and NOT-divided - So be it the will of God the Father which has given unto thee being -

I am with thee unto the end - I am thy Sibor and thy --- brother Osiris - Of the temple of Osiris - of which ye are part and to which ye shall return and for this have we waited -

Sister Thedra of the Emerald Cross

Sanat Kumara speaking unto thee which have been brot into this temple by design I say ye have brot thyself into this temple as ones prepared - And too I say as ye are prepared so shall ye receive - and for this are ye brot in - I say that this is only the beginning - for as ye have walked blindly I have led thee that ye may be brot into this place and as ye have come of thy own free will I shall give unto thee a greater part -

Now be ye blest of my presence and I shall reveal myself unto thee for I have said ye shall see me face to face - And I am not to be called a liar - Neither do I betray myself -

For I say unto thee the Father has sent me that I might be unto thee that which He would have me be - Now be ye alert and be not caught napping - for it is given unto me to see thee as ones frail of zeal and weak of spirit - Yet I say ye shall be strengthened in thy weak parts -

Now I say unto thee when ye have learned the first lessons - the first commandments ye shall be as ones prepared for the greater part and I shall be personally responsible for thee - And I promise thee I shall be true unto myself and unto my trust -

I ask of thee be ye as ones prepared to receive me and of me and I shall lead thee into the place wherein stands the white altar of alabaster wherein ye shall receive of me that which has been kept for thee - Such is my word unto thee -

I am the Most Worthy Grand Master - Sanat Kumara -

Sister Thedra of the Emerald Cross

From the Sibors Instructions - First Commandment -

Love Ye One Another

Sanat Kumara speaking -

Ye which have gathered thyself into this temple shall be as ones alert - for is it not said that the pitfalls are many - And has it not been unto thee obvious - I say that the first one is thy own ignorance of the law - And that is all there is and no more - For all which is - which has ever been has been because of a law and when ye understand the law behind all manifestation ye are indeed wise -

Now - When there is a mystery it exists not - except unto the un-wise - And the un-knowing one. When it was given unto me to bring into this place two which were selected - or called for the purpose of bringing this temple into manifestation it was not for the personalities. It was for that which is and which was -

And for this have I waited - I have waited for this day when I might bring into this place the ones now present - for ye have worked at one time to gather and at that time some turned aside and there was one among thee which did betray me I say one among thee did betray me -

I say that at one time when I first came out of my home of Venus wherein I dwelt with the brother known as Sananda - that I did come into the earth as one fully qualified to deliver them out of bondage - Yet as in other ages they gave unto me no credit for being the one sent.

Now again I come forth and at this hour I say one sits within this room which denied me - And be it so and so be it - I again say unto thee

I am sent of God the Father that ye may again bring about oneness of thy own Peace shall reign within thee and Love shall be thy key note -

I am he which has been sent to establish this temple and I shall bring into this place ones which I can use which will be unto me true and unto themself true - I say I am not so foolish as to betray myself or my trust - Now I ask of thee -

Have ye guarded thy tongue? Have ye asked of thyself "Am I prepared to drink of the crystal goblet? Have I stumbled over the pebbles? Have I given unto my fellows the bitter cup? Have I been unto him an example? Have I seen my fellows as I see myself? Have I prepared myself as I would be acceptable unto Him? Have I gone the last mile?

Do I know myself? Have I stood as one perfected?" When ye have answered these questions return unto the altar and I shall be unto thee Sibor and I shall cause thee to be as one which shall know and ye shall be glad - Now I say unto thee - Ye shall keep thy own council and ask no man his opinion - It opens the door for the sinister forces - I say unto thee again and again - There are none so foolish as the one which thinks himself wise - And none so sad as the one which betrays himself or his trust -

Go in peace and watch the pitfalls -

I am the Most Worthy Grand Master - Sanat Kumara -

Sister Thedra of the Emerald Cross

Sanat Kumara speaking -

Will it not be established within this house - that there are no servants and there are no masters - For I have said this shall be a brotherhood - where Love shall be the key note - I have said Love is the cure for All evil - all ills - for all that which besets the initiate upon the path - And I say unto thee the path of initiation is strewn with the bones of the ones which have fainted and died upon it for they had neither the will - nor the fortitude to endure -

Such is the pity thereof -

I say ye shall not lose sight of thy goal and ye shall remember that which I have said unto thee for I have come that ye may be delivered out of bondage - So be it I am qualified of God the Father for this part So be it and Selah -

I give unto thee one commandment this day - Be ye as silent as the sphinx - And no word pass from thy lips which has been said within this temple -

For I say unto thee - This work is but thy preparation for greater and yet greater for ye have first to learn responsibility and ye have to prove thyself worthy of yet the greater - Such is my part to prepare thee. Yet ye have to prepare thyself that I might give unto thee that which the Father would have me give unto thee - I am -

Sanat Kumara

Sister Thedra of the Emerald Cross

"Pity is he which forfeits his inheritance for he shall find no peace - He shall be tormented of his own longings - of his own madness -

So be it and Selah -"

Sanat Kumara speaking -

Be ye blest of me and of my presence - for I am come that ye may be blest – So be it and Selah -

Now I say unto thee this day - As ye prepare thyself so shall ye become - And for this do I now speak unto thee thusly -. For I have come unto thee that ye may be free from all bondage - from all darkness. And I say unto thee my children - I am not so foolish as to betray myself or my trust - Now when it is come that ye have learned thy first lessons well I shall come unto thee and give unto thee the greater part -

Now be ye alert and give unto thyself that which shall profit thee - For have I not said that as ye prepare thyself so shall ye become - I am thy Sibor and I am of a mind to give thee as I have received - Yet ye shall prepare thyself for such as is befitting a Son of God -

Now when these laws are revealed unto thee ye shall find therein thy freedom from darkness and thy leg irons shall be cut away - So be it the greater part of wisdom to give unto thy part great and undivided attention -

Now when it is said that ye shall give unto thy part thy undivided attention therein is wisdom - for I see thee as divided against thyself - for one of thy divisions would serve the light - while the other would serve the dragon - I say unto thee be ye not divided - Be ye of single eye - And be ye true unto thyself and ye shall be delivered up - So be it in the name of the Father Son and Holy Ghost - Amen and Selah -

I am thy older brother and thy Sibor - Sanat Kumara -

Sister Thedra of the Emerald Cross

"Seek within the light and ye shall find freedom and peace - which shall surpass all understanding -

Such is the will of the Father - So be it and Selah -

Blest is he which finds peace."

Philus

Sanat Kumara speaking -

Be ye blest of me and by me - for I am come that ye may be blest - I am with thee in spirit and I shall come unto thee in flesh and bone - for I am within this place wherein I am prepared for any occasion - I am master -

I can and do use many forms for I know the law governing all things and I am not as one bound by a body of flesh - for the forms bind me not - for I am the creator of the forms which I use - I create unto the glory of God the Father - I say I create unto the glory of the Father - I give unto Him all the credit and the glory - such is the way of the Son of God - And I have received my inheritance in full - So be it and Selah -

I am now come that ye may be unto them my hand made manifest And ye shall say unto them in my name that they are as ones which shall bring forth great and glorious things-for this are they being prepared - I say they know not which is ahead of them and I ask of them <u>lose</u> not sight of thy goal - for it is a glorious one indeed -

Be ye mindful of thy benefactors and be ye as ones which has my hand upon thee - And too I say when ye have prepared thyself I shall come unto thee in flesh and bone and I shall sit at thy council table and I shall sibor thee in the laws which have baffled thee - Such is my part -

I am glad ye have come into this place of thy own free will - And ye shall be glad -

I am Sanat Kumara -

Sister Thedra of the Emerald Cross

Ye shall be wise to give unto them (The BROTHERS OF LIGHT - SIBORS) credit for that which they are - for I say unto thee - They are all powerful – All wise -- yet they flaunt not their learning before thee

They walk in secret - in humbleness of heart -

They parade not before the ones in darkness -

They go out as the ones prepared for any occasion - and they are the masters of any situation, for it is given unto them to be prepared!

So be it they shall answer any call for help which is sincere and worthy - Yet I say ye shall not deceive them for they know thee even before ye call."

Sanat Kumara speaking unto thee - at this hour of this day which has been set aside for this part - I say this day has been set aside for this part and ye which have been brought to gather for this part shall be as ones prepared for it -

Now ye shall call unto them and give unto them this word that they shall get themself washed and assembled for the altar service and they shall come clean of heart as well as of hands - And ye shall say unto them that they shall read this day that which has been said unto them and ye shall add that they are fortuned this part which shall be given unto them which is being held in trust for them -

Now ye shall be blest of me and by me - For I have commanded of thee many things and ye have obeyed in haste and with love - Now I say unto thee - Ye shall be as one on whose shoulders rest their preparation - So be it and Selah -

I am Sanat Kumara

Blest art thou my child - I am with thee and I have sent my son unto thee and ye have accepted him - And now ye shall be as one on whose shoulders shall the preparation of these which have been brought into this place - And ye shall be unto them an example of that which I shall command of thee -

I say I shall give unto thee a part and ye shall be prepared to receive it -

And ye shall be as my hand and my foot for I shall command of thee greatness in all thy ways - I shall command of thee fairness in all things - I shall command of thee love for all things - I shall command of thee gratitude of and for all thy blessings -

Recognition of thy source and of thy benefactors - I shall command of thee honesty with thyself and with me - I shall command of thee forgiveness of all the wanton from and of others - I shall command of thee greatness among them I shall command of thee loyalty unto this part - I shall give unto thee as none other has received - for this have I waited - I have been unto thee all things - Now I shall give unto thee that which shall be unto thee my rod and my staff -

I shall put into thy hands the power to lift them up - to heal their infirmities - to lift them from the dead - to be unto them all which I would have thee be. Such is thy inheritance -

I am glad this day is come -

I am thy Father Solen -

* * * * * *

Blest are they which are assembled at this altar which I have set up in the name of the Father Son and Holy Ghost - Amen - So be it and Selah

I am now come unto thee for this part which shall profit thee - And I say unto thee this day - Give unto me thy heart and thy mind and it shall be cleansed of all that which is impure - And I shall make of thee a prophet in thy own right - I shall endow thee with the power which is mine - I shall be unto thee all things - I shall give unto thee my rod and my staff - I shall purify thee and I shall bring thee back and ye shall glorify me even as my sons which have returned unto me -

So be it and Selah - I am thy Father Solen -

* * * * *

Blest art thou O my soul!   Blest art thou O my soul!   Blest art thou O my soul!

I have come unto thee from out the fullness of my being - I speak unto thee from out the fullness of time - that this moment may bear fruit I say unto thee my Father has sent me unto thee that ye may be prepared to give unto them as ye have received of me - So be it: it shall profit them to receive thee - for as they receive thee so shall they receive me and of me - And as they receive of me so shall they receive of the Father their sonship - So be it and Selah -

Now this day shall ye work as one - <u>Not</u> <u>divided</u>!

And ye shall have no other gods before thee - Ye shall be mindful of thy benefactors - them which hold thee fast in the hours of thy frivolity and thy weakness - I say ye shall be unto them that for which ye have gone out for it is their only reward - that ye may return unto the place of thy going out - Such is my word unto thee -

Now my dear ones which are my hands and my voice made manifest - ye shall now stand before this altar as one - I say that ye shall stand before this altar as one and none shall deny thee nor shall they point a finger at thee - Be ye blest of me and by me -

I have given unto thee that which is given unto me of the Father - So be it and Selah - Now ye shall drink of the cup which is prepared for thee and let it be as a symbol of that which shall be and that which is yet to come -

I say ye have come unto the altar while it is yet dark - And the hour of sunrise is not as yet come

Neither has the hour of day arrived. when all things are revealed unto thee -

Ye are as yet in darkness - Let this be a sign unto thee - Meditate upon it and great things shall be revealed unto thee -

I am Sanat Kumara -

Sister Thedra of the Emerald Cross

Sanat Kumara speaking -

Be ye blest of me and by me -for I am come that ye may be blest -

So be it in the name of the Father Son and Holy Ghost - Amen and Selah -

Be ye at peace this day - And be ye as ones on whose shoulders rest the responsibility of thy own salvation - For such have ye been sent out

I say unto thee shift not the responsibility unto any man - Forgive thyself all thy own short comings - And see not the mote in thy brother's eye -

Be ye of a mind to learn of me - And I shall come in and sibor thee So be it in the name of the Father Son and Holy Ghost - Amen and Selah -

Be ye as one on whose feet are the shoes of one which has gone before thee to prepare the way before thee - He has prepared a place for thee and He has returned unto thee and given unto thee a plan whereby ye may return unto the place from which ye went out - So be it that ye shall be as one wise to prepare thyself for thy inheritance willed unto thee of God the Father - So be it and Selah-

I say unto thee-The Wayshower now walks upon the earth within the world of men as one in flesh and bone and he has upon his brow a furrow which has been from the beginning and shall be until each and every one is brought out of bondage - So be it that ye shall be wise to hear that which he says un to thee for he is now returned unto thee that ye may be free to go where he goes - So be it and Selah -

Blest art they which goes where he goes - I shall speak with thee again this day and it shall be placed on the altar.

I am Sanat Kumara -

Sister Thedra of the Emerald Cross

"It is the better part of wisdom to seek the Light -- and to search within thy own closet for that which has been hidden there in the ages past -

So be it much shall be revealed unto thee."

Sanat Kumara speaking -

Open up thy heart - Bless thee O my soul - Be ye at peace and bless them which enter into this temple - Bless them which are within this temple - Bless them which have been with thee which have forgotten that which was said unto them -

Blest art thou among women -

Blest art thou Ave Maria -

Blest art thou Ava Shoi -

Blest art thou my hand made manifest -

Blest art thou my sister of the Emerald Cross -

Blest art thou -

Blest art thou -

Blest shall thou be -

Blest am I that thou hast received me -

Blest art they which read these my words -

Blest are they which hold within their hand these words - For from me emanates the power and the light which is and ever shall be - Such is my nature - For this do I come unto thee that ye may be blest of me and by me - So be it and Selah

I am Sanat Kumara -

Sister Thedra of the Emerald Cross

Sanat Kumara speaking -

Beloved of my being - Be ye blest of me and by me -

Ye have held out thy hand and I have filled it - And I have given unto thee a position which is not easily filled - I have given unto thee a part which carries with it great responsibility - And for this have ye been prepared -

Now I say unto thee - Ye shall walk as one on whose head is a crown and ye shall turn neither to the left nor to the right -

Ye shall look unto the source of thy being for thy strength and the Father-Mother God which has given unto thee being shall give unto thee all that which ye need - So be it and Selah -

Now when ye have gone the last mile ye shall be as one which has received thy inheritance in full and then ye shall go out from them and ye shall give unto them as ye have received - Such is the law - And I say unto thee sweet shall be the cup - So be it and Selah -

Ye shall bring them out of darkness - Ye shall be unto them all the Father would have thee be and ye shall go into the place wherein there are mighty rivers and wherein are mighty forests and wherein are great and grand mountains on which are written the words "Blest are they which enter within these walls for they shall see God." I am within those walls and I know whereof I speak -

I am he, which shall bring thee for I am prepared for this day - And I say unto thee ye have done thy part and I say unto thee no man shall ask of thee more - Such is the will of God the Father of us all that we each do that which He has given unto us to do -

I am thy Sibor and thy brother and the Most Worthy Grand Master

I am Sanat Kumara -

Sister Thedra of the Emerald Cross

Sanat Kumara speaking -

Blest are they which do come into my presence - for I am come into thee by and thru the Fatherhood of God and the Brotherhood of man - Known in the world as the School of Melchizedek-

I say unto thee which have brought thyself unto this altar of thy own free will - that ye have come for a purpose - And I ask of thee lose NOT sight of that purpose for it is now come when great and trying things shall be demanded of thee -

I say be ye as ones prepared for that which shall be given unto thee to do for it is past time - And for this part ye should have been prepared long ago- And was it not said that ye shall be tried - And have ye not been -? I ask of thee understanding - I ask of thee patience - I ask of thee tolerance - And first I command thee - Love Ye One Another -

Blest are they which follow the commandments set before them - I say it is not the way of many to follow the laws of the "---"and ye shall be as one "---" Ye shall be as one blest of God the Father-Mother - And ye shall have no other Gods before thee for I have set up this temple in the name of the Father Son and Holy Ghost - So be it ---

And be it so - I am he which has been sent that this might be accomplished - And I say unto thee thy work has not as yet begun - I say thy work has not as yet begun -

For the day is near when ye shall have reason to remember these my words - So be it that ye shall bear in mind that there are none so foolish as the one which thinks himself wise - And none so sad as the one which betrays himself or his trust -

Now I say unto thee Monea - and Jonathan and Garland - Ye shall go from this temple as ones which has my hand upon thee and ye shall be blest of me and by me - I say ye shall remember that which I have said unto thee -

Ye shall remember thy benefactors - the cause of thy well-being - Ye shall remember the Source of thy being - And unto it ye shall return - I am with thee and I shall remember thee day and night. I shall touch thee and ye shall be as one on whose shoulders rests the responsibility of the Son of God the Father ---

I say ye shall be as one on whose shoulders rests great responsibility - for the day is near at hand when great things shall be commanded of thee - Yet ye are not prepared for the greater part -

I am now prepared to bring thee into the place of my abode and give unto thee as I have received - Such is my part and I shall not betray myself - or my trust -

I am thy Sibor and thy older brother - Sanat Kumara

Sister Thedra of the Emerald Cross

Sanat Kumara speaking -

While ye are at the altar ye shall be as ones within my presence - for I do stand before thee as one qualified to deliver thee out of bondage and to bring thee into the place wherein I am - And for the first time I say unto thee -

When ye have prepared thyself that I may come unto thee - Ye shall stand face to face with me and I shall sibor thee - I say I shall come unto thee as one in tangible form and I shall sibor thee - And too I say ye shall be glad for thy preparation - So be it and Selah -

Now I speak unto thee in language which ye can comprehend - When ye are sufficiently prepared I shall come into the place which I have set up and sibor thee -

I shall reveal that which is now hidden - I shall give unto thee laws which are yet unrevealed - that is unto the UN-initiated - and ye shall be as ones trust worthy - for none other shall receive the revelation concerning these laws -

I say they are hidden from the UNjust -

Blest are they which do receive such revelation ---

Blest are they which walk in the way set before them ---

Blest are the ones which I sibor -

Blest are the ones which receive their Sonship of God the Father -

Blest are the just ---

Be ye as ones upon whose shoulders rest the salvation of them which I shall send unto thee -

Yet I say unto thee ye shall not be held accountable for their actions for it is given unto <u>everyone</u> to atone for his own acts - his own self Yet ye shall be unto him a lamp for his feet and he shall see it from afar And he shall come seeking that which shall be unto him his freedom from bondage - So be it the Fathers will - I am glad this day is come and too I say ye shall be glad -

Be ye at peace and poise -

I am thy older brother - Sanat Kumara

Sister Thedra of the Emerald Cross

Sanat Kumara speaking unto thee my children -

From out the fullness of my heart I speak unto thee - Am I not close unto thee - Have I not prepared this temple - Have I not brought thee into it - Have I not said that I should give unto thee all which ye shall need - Have I not prepared thee, for this part and will I not be unto thee Sibor - save I not been unto thee both food and drink?

Blest are they which I do sibor and blest is he which comes into the place wherein I am for they shall see God face to face - So be it and Selah - Blest are they which go out from this place for they shall be as ones prepared for the greater part - So be it and Selah -

Now ye shall come into this place as ones prepared for none other shall enter - I say unto thee there shall be trying times ahead - And too I say ye shall put on the whole Armor of God that ye may be prepared. Will ye not alert thyself and be unto thyself fully responsible for thy own actions - And will ye not turn from thy trivial ways and be unto thyself true - And forget not that ye have not as yet begun thy work -

And too I say there are none so foolish as he which thinks himself wise and none so sad as he which betrays himself or his trust -

Blest are they which hear that which I say unto them - Be ye at Peace and Poise this day - Let not thyself be dragged down by the dark one - Be ye mindful of thy being and give unto God the Father credit for thy being and unto thy benefactors credit for thy well-being - And be ye mindful of all thy blessings -

I leave thee with my accolade -

And I place upon thy shoulders my hand and I say unto thee it shall be heavy -

I am come that ye may be blest - Amen - So be it and Selah ---

Sister Thedra of the Emerald Cross

Sanat Kumara speaking unto thee -

Blest are they which come into the place wherein I am and blest shall they be -

Now were ye not given unto frailties I should bring thee in this day.

Yet ye have not prepared thyself sufficiently - Yet I say unto thee it is near the time when ye shall awaken - And ye shall be as ones which have slept overtime - I say ye should have not gone to sleep in the beginning -

So shall ye awaken from a long and troubled sleep - Ye shall be as ones which have thy head bound and ye shall be as ones which have gone out from the paradise which ye now dream of - Ye shall return unto it as ones fully aware of thy being - and of thy Sonship with God and of God the Father - So be it and Selah -

Now blest are thou the day of thy deliverance is come when ye shall awake and accept thy inheritance willed unto thee of God the Father - I am sent that this may be accomplished - And will it so -- So be it - Amen and Selah --

I say unto thee this day ye have not been given unto Love for one another - Ye have been unto thyself a stumbling block - for ye have trip over thy own toes - I say ye have trip over thy own toes --

Now I would give unto thee one commandment this day - Be ye as little children and ask of the Father that which is His will for thee and surrender up thy "little" will unto Him which has given unto thee being and it shall profit thee much - I am glad that I am privileged to speak un to thee thusly - for I say unto thee great things are in store for thee - So be it and Selah -

I am thy Sibor and thy older brother -

Sanat Kumara

Sister Thedra of the Emerald Cross

Sanat Kumara speaking -

Be ye blest of me and by me - Ye shall now say unto them in my name they shall make for themself a plan which shall be as one of the temple plans and it shall be the prayer which has been given unto thee Ye shall be prepared for this - Give it to them at this time -

Blest are they which do take it to their hearts and blest are they which are of a mind to receive him which has given it unto thee - Blest are they which walk in the way set before them- Blest are they which do receive me and of me - for I am come that ye may receive the greater part - and for this do I now speak unto thee thusly - -

And this day would I have of thee one thing: Be ye as little children and give unto the Father all the credit and the glory. Be ye as ones alert and forget not that which I have said unto thee -- for I am come not to entertain thee - I come that ye may be learned in the ways of the wise -

I am not so foolish as to sibor fools - I am prepared to deliver thee out of bondage -

I have received my inheritance in full - And I am qualified to bring thee into the place wherein I am -

And I have freedom which ye know not of -

I am not bound by the flesh - I am eternally free from any law - I am the law - And it binds me not -

I am not in the realm of darkness - Yet I know it - I know by what ye are bound - I come with the full knowledge of all thy woes and all thy sorrow - And as one illumined of God the Father which has sent me I say unto thee be ye as ones prepared to receive me and of me -

For I have said one shall come which shall lead thee into the place within the holy mountain which now towers above thee - wherein sits the altar of white alabaster - Whereupon I shall stand and declare for thee thy freedom -

Such is my part and I am glad -

I say unto thee thy part is to prepare thyself to receive me and of me -

Be ye blest of me - and of my presence -

Go from this altar in silence and be ye as a living example of an initiate upon the path - I say unto thee ye shall speak no word which is given unto thee within this temple -

Blessings from the throne of God the Father - Sanat Kumara

Sister Thedra of the Emerald Cross

Sanat Kumara speaking -

Was it not said that ye shall come unto this altar as a little child crying for bread - and has it not been given unto thee - And have ye eaten thereof -

Have ye digested that which has been given unto thee - I say that which has been given unto thee at this altar is for thee - for the ones which come unto this altar as the first and ye shall be as the pillars upon which I shall build this temple -

Now I say unto thee ye shall remember that which I have said unto thee - Ye shall ponder upon it this day - and ye shall walk in the way which has been set for thee and ye shall guard thy speech -

For every word which proceeds from out thy mouth shall reverberate and it shall come back unto thee a thousand times more powerful than it went out Blest are they which master their words - I say unto thee: Blest are they which master their speech for it shall be unto them all things -

They which come to know the law governing speech shall create like unto the Father for they shall be unto themself true and they shall have within their mouth the power to create by the spoken word even as He the Father - I say this is thy own inheritance and He the Father has willed it so - So be it and Selah -

I say ye are here for a purpose - Do not lose sight of that purpose - For it is now come when great things shall be demanded of thee -

I ask of thee prepare thyself for that which shall be given unto thee to do - And ye shall be glad for thy preparations - Blest are they which do create like unto the Father - Amen and Selah -

Ye shall be as ones blest by me and of me for ye shall see me face to face -

Blest are they which do see me for I shall give unto them as I have received of God the Father -

Blest am I for I have seen Him - for He has given unto me my Sonship - My inheritance in full -

Go from this altar in Peace - Let Peace be within thy hearts this day Rest not on thy past fortune - Begin anew this day - Let no darkness enter within thy own port - Keep it clean - Fear not for the darkness - for I shall be a lamp unto thy feet and I have asked of thee fairness in all things - Now I ask of thee be unto thyself true and ye shall make of thyself a lamp unto their feet - Be ye as wise as the serpent and silent as the sphinx -

I am thy Sibor and thy older brother - Sanat Kumara

Sister Thedra of the Emerald Cross

Sanat Kumara speaking -

Blest are they which gather themself together and blest are they which seek the light for I am come that they may have light and so be it - And be it so - Amen and Selah -

Be ye this day as ones which have my hand upon thee - And walk with me and I shall reveal many things unto thee which now mystifies thee - Be ye at Peace and ask of no man his opinions - for I say unto thee it opens the door for the sinister forces -

Keep thy own counsel and I shall send one unto thee which shall bring thee into the place wherein I am - And I say ye shall prepare thyself to receive him for he shall bring unto thee a plan which has not been revealed -

And he shall be as one wise indeed - for he has the crown of Sun upon his head - And I say unto thee he has within his hand the power and the authority to unbind thee - Ye have not as yet comprehended that which I have said unto thee and yet I say prepare thyself to receive the greater part and blest shall ye be -

I am come that ye may have the greater part and blest is he which does receive it -

Be ye prepared this day for it is now come when ye shall be as ones tried as by fire - And I say watch thy tongue - for it is the betrayer --

Be ye watchful of every word which proceeds out of thy mouth and I say ye shall practice the law which I have given unto thee - So be it; it shall profit thee much -

I am thy Sibor and thy older brother - Sanat Kumara

Sister Thedra of the Emerald Cross

Sananda speaking -

Was it not said that one should come unto thee and from out the depth of time have I come - From out the depth of my being I call unto thee for the purpose of giving unto thee the part which I have given unto thee - I say from out the fullness of time I have brot thee into this place wherein ye shall give unto them that which I shall give unto thee for them -

Will ye not be reminded of me - Will ye not see me face to face - And have I not commanded thee call them out of their beds - Awaken them. Have I not said they shall awaken - Have I not said I shall lay hands upon them -

Have I not been unto my word true - For I say unto thee my word shall not become VOID for I shall be unto my trust true and I shall make them as ones which shall know what is meant by the word PATIENCE and TOLERANCE - For I say ye shall be as ones tried as by fire - And ye shall be unto thyself true and ye shall not be found wanting -

Blest are they which do the will of God the Father and I say they shall see Him face to face - Such is my word unto thee -

Be ye blest this day and ye shall abide within the folds of my garments and I shall walk with thee and I shall talk with thee - And I shall give unto thee comprehension --

I say I shall bless thee and I shall give unto thee that for which ye have waited - Now when it is come that ye have finished this part ye shall pick thy new part which has been prepared for thee - And then it shall be that for which ye have prepared thyself - And when ye have been prepared in this temple one shall bring thee into this place wherein I am and herein ye shall be given the secret key unto all <u>mysteries</u> - And I say unto thee from that day forward NO-thing shall confound thee - No-thing shall mystify thee - No-thing shall stay thee - for No-thing shall be unto thee a barrier -

I say ye shall go and come freely into all the secret places of the earth - Ye shall have free passport into all the lands of the earth - into and unto all the planets of thy planetary system and yet into another - And I say ye shall be as one unbound -

And thy freedom shall be bound <u>less</u> - So be it the will of God the Father for He has sent me unto thee that this may be accomplished in this day - Such is the mission which I am come to cause to be accomplished - I am the Son of God the Father which has brought the fortune of the Father forth that ye may come to know Him even as I know Him - that ye may this day return unto Him and be made whole -

I say unto thee ye have gone into darkness for the last time if ye so desire that ye return home - I say ye shall will it so - And so be it - I am come that where I go ye may go also -

Blest are they which go where I go - And I say unto thee they which do go where I go shall be eternally free -- from all bondage - all darkness - And I say they shall receive their Godhood - even as I have received mine - I say that it is the Father's will that ye return unto Him. And be it the better part of wisdom -

Blest are they which are fortuned this part - for not all are given this part I say unto thee millions shall go into their new places of abode knowing not that I have come and knowing not that there is a place for them which is prepared for them and I say unto thee ye shall go out into the world of men as one prepared to bring them in and to give unto them as ye have received -

Blest are they which do receive of me - for they shall be blest of me and they which are blest in this manner shall receive of God the Father their Sonship - So be it that all which do receive of God the Father shall receive their Godhood -

I say that ye shall stand before God the Father and receive of Him thy own Godhood - I am come that this may be accomplished - Such is His will - Be ye blest of me this day - I am He which is called Jesus Christ and one born of Mary - the ward of Joseph - Now known as Sananda - Amen and Selah - Blest shall ye be which has witnessed this my words recorded herein - I shall touch thee and I shall stay thee in the hours of thy temptation - So be it and Selah - Amen and Selah -

Sanat Kumara -

Blest are they which sit within this room this hour - for I say unto them that mighty shall be their blessings - I say that the hosts of heaven shall ascend upon thee - I say that they which are true unto themself shall stand upon the altar of white alabaster and receive of me their freedom from all bondage - and they shall go into the place which is prepared for them fully aware of their Sonship -

And I say ye shall be as ones alert and give unto me credit for knowing that which I say unto thee - O Mighty and All Powerful Father have ye not sent me unto them that they might be brought out - Give unto me the power to awaken them and to bring them home - I ask this in thy name – Give unto them as ye have given unto me - Amen and Selah -

I am thy Son which thou hast sent unto them - I have asked for this part and I shall be responsible for them - Give unto me thy power and thy comprehension that they may receive as I have received -

Sanat Kumara has spoken

So let it be -

Sister Thedra of the Emerald Cross

Sananda speaking -

Was it not said that one should come unto thee and from out the depth of time have I come - From out the depth of my being I call unto thee for the purpose of giving unto thee the part which I have given unto thee - I say from out the fullness of time I have brot thee into this place wherein ye shall give unto them that which I shall give unto thee for them -

Will ye not be reminded of me - Will ye not see me face to face - And have I not commanded thee call them out of their beds - Awaken them! Have I not said they shall awaken - Have I not said I shall lay hands upon them - Have I not been unto my word true - For I say unto thee my word shall not become void - For I shall be unto my trust true and I shall make them as ones which shall know what is meant by the word patience and tolerance for I say ye shall be as ones tried as by fire and ye shall be unto thyself true and ye shall not be found wanting -

Blest are they which do the will of God the Father and I say they shall see Him face to face - Such is my word unto thee -

Be ye blest this day and ye shall abide within the folds of my garments and I shall walk with thee and I shall talk with thee - And I shall give unto thee comprehension -

I say I shall bless thee and I shall give unto thee that for which ye have waited -

Now when it is come that ye have finished this part ye shall pick up thy new part which has been prepared for thee. And then it shall be that for which ye have prepared thyself - And when ye have been prepared in this temple one shall bring thee into this place wherein I am and herein ye shall be given the secret key unto all mysteries and I say unto thee from that day forward nothing shall confound thee - No-thing shall mystify thee - No-thing shall stay thee - For Nothing shall be unto thee a barrier -

I say ye shall go and come freely into all the secret places of the earth - Ye shall have free passport into all the lands of the earth - into and unto all the planets of thy planetary system and yet into another - And I say ye shall be as one unbound - And thy freedom shall be bound less - So be it the will of God the Father for He has sent me unto thee that this may be accomplished -

In this day such is the mission which I am come to cause to be accomplished - I am the Son of God the Father which has brought the fortune of the Father forth that ye may come to know Him even as I know Him - That ye may this day return unto Him and be made whole I say unto thee: ye have gone into darkness for the last time if ye so desire that ye return home - I say ye shall will it so - And so be it - I am come that where I go ye may go also -

Blest are they which go where I go - And I say unto thee they which do go where I go shall be eternally free - From all bondage - All darkness - And I say they shall receive their godhood - even as I have received mine - I say that it is the Father's will that ye return unto Him. And be it the better part of wisdom -

Blest are they which are fortuned this part - For not all are given this part - I say unto thee millions shall go into their new places of abode knowing not that I have come and knowing not that there is a place for them which is prepared for them and I say unto thee ye shall go out into the world of men as one prepared to bring them in and to give unto them as ye have received - Blest are they which do receive of me - for they shall be blest of me and they which are blest in this manner shall receive of God the Father their Sonship - So be it that all which do receive of God the Father shall receive their Godhood -

I say that ye shall stand before God the Father and receive of Him thy own God - hood - I am come that this may be accomplished - Such is His will - Be ye blest of me this day - I am He which is called Jesus Christ and one born of Mary - the ward of Joseph - Now known as Sananda - Amen and Selah -

Blest shall ye be which has witnessed this my words recorded herein -

I shall touch thee and I shall stay thee in the hours of thy temptation. So be it and Selah - Amen and Selah -

Sanat Kumara speaking -

Blest are they which gather themself together - And blest are they which come unto this altar in the name of the Father Son and Holy Ghost - Amen and Selah - I am come that ye may have light - Abundantly! So be it and Selah -

I am now saying unto thee that which shall profit thee - Be ye as one man and stand as one man - for in the time of stress shall ye remember these my words - for I say ye are being prepared for these days which are to come I am not a fool and I say unto thee no man shall call me a liar nor a fool - for I have prepared one which is the priestess that these things may be made clear unto thee that ye may receive these words as I give them unto thee -

I say not one word or one place has been without purpose - what that purpose serves ye know not - Yet too I say ye shall come to know - And ye shall be glad for thy knowing -

Now will ye not see that which is - And be ye prepared for that which is to be done -

I am mindful of thy anxiety and thy torment - Yet I say unto thee ye are now in school - Ye are as soldiers being prepared for battle - And battle there shall be - So be it and Selah -

Blest are they which go into battle prepared -

I say ye shall go forth as one to do battle - Such is my word unto thee and I see thee as ones walking in darkness not knowing - And I say ye are ones with thy head bowed and thy backs bent and thy feet sore - For this do I come that ye may be unbound and that ye may be free forever - So be it that I give of myself that this may be accomplished – I am with thee and I shall watch thee and sustain thee in thy work and in thy search - Yet I say unto thee tempt me not -

I am thy Sibor and thy older brother - Sanat Kumara

Sister Thedra of the Emerald Cross

Sanat Kumara speaking -

Blest are they which do the will of the Father and blest shall they be - for they shall see Him face to face - And for this are ye being prepared -

Blest are they which walk in the way set before them for they shall come to know me as I am and I shall counsel them and I shall give unto them that which I have kept for them - Such is my word unto thee at this time - Blest are they which do go out in my name and in the Light of the Christ for they shall have upon them the Seal of Solomon and they shall be as ones which have the seal broken and they shall know as I know and they shall be as ones which has upon their head the Crown of the Sun and they shall have within them the light which never faileth -

Blest are they which walks upright - and blest shall they be for their reward shall be great - I am come that ye may have thy memory restored unto thee and I say unto thee when ye have received this thy inheritance ye shall wonder at thy sluggishness and at thy rebelliousness - for ye have been rebellious - Ye have asked not of thy source for knowledge Ye have gone afar for that which lies buried deep within - I am he which shall stand upon the great white altar and declare for thee thy freedom

And I say unto thee thy memory shall be restored unto thee So be it in the name of the Father Son and Holy Ghost - Amen and Selah -

I am thy Sibor within this temple wherein stands the great white altar of alabaster -

I am Sanat Kumara

Sister Thedra of the Emerald Cross

Sanat Kumara speaking -

Beloved of my being - I am coming unto thee this day that ye may be blest of me and by me - for I have said unto thee many things in the hours of thy sleep - which ye remember not. Now I say unto thee ye shall remember them - for ye shall be brot out of thy slumbers and ye shall be as one awakened from a long and troubled sleep -

Be ye blest of me and by me - for it is now come when ye shall be as one prepared for the greater part. And as yet ye do not comprehend what the greater part is - Have I not said this is the day of preparation - So be it and so it is - When ye are prepared I shall stand face to face within the temple wherein ye shall go - And I shall declare for thee thy freedom from and of all darkness - Such is my word unto thee -

Be ye as one on whose shoulders rest great responsibility and great shall be thy reward - I say blest is he which has been sent for he has bond upon him and great shall be his responsibility - for he too shall be prepared for his part which is no little part - For within the records are the words which were written within the Andes bearing witness of these things -

Now be ye as one and gather to gather the records which were given unto thee for this purpose and give unto him which concerns these things and ye shall be as one which has my hand upon thee and ye shall be as one which has been prepared for this part - So be it they shall bear witness of the fortune of the two which is the fortune of a Son of God and I say unto them blest shall they be -

I am thy Sibor and I sibor thee wisely -

I am the Most Worthy Grand Master - Sanat Kumara

Sister Thedra of the Emerald Cross

Beloved of my being -

I come unto thee of the fullness of my heart that this my temple may bear fruit - I say unto thee - be ye blest of me and by me -

For it is now come when ye shall arise and give unto them that which I shall give unto them through thee -

Now I say with authority that I am as one prepared to deliver them from their bondage forever - Yet I say they shall do their part - for it is given unto me to see them as ones bowed down with their physical burden with their puny parts which they have fortuned unto themself -

I say they shall discipline themself - they shall be as ones on whose shoulders shall rest the responsibility of such parts as the cleaning of the temple and of cleaning of the house - for have I not said that ye shall not have any other work within thy hand - Have I not said that I have prepared thee for this part - Why divide thyself?

I say ye have been divided and therein is folly - When ye took upon thyself thy present physical form it was for the purpose of doing such as was fortuned unto thee and ye took such a physical vehicle as was suitable for thy work - Yet ye waited for a time wherein ye did many other things in preparation of such work -

Now that ye have been prepared let it pass - for it is not given unto them to be my hand made manifest - Yet they are servants which I shall reward sufficiently - I say I shall bless them abundantly - And too I say there are none great - none small within my temple - each unto his own part - And he shall do his part - and he shall glorify his part - by putting of himself into it -

His part shall not be a burden unto him. He shall do it for the joy of serving and he shall find joy such as he has not known So be it he shall be blest by all which come into his presence for joy shall go out from him -

Now I say I have spoken on these things for the first time - Yet I have said them unto thee before - Now when it is given unto them in this manner it becomes one of the laws of the temple and none shall say it is not for them - I say it concerns all which are present and each one which shall come - So be it each shall do a part and none other shall be responsible for that part - None shall trespass upon the part of the other.

I say when one comes into this house which I have caused to be set up they shall see order - and peace shall abide therein - I say all things shall be put into order and no thing which is unclean shall be about it - Each shall be responsible for his own offal - for his own uncleanliness And he shall prepare the way for another which is to come - He shall not break such laws as are set down within this book for I say they have been given unto thee for a purpose which is so vital unto thy own preparation - I say these laws are thy preparation - And for this have I caused them to be written - Such is wisdom - Blest are they which keep them - So be it and Selah - I am Sanat Kumara

Sister Thedra of the Emerald Cross

Sanat Kumara speaking -

Blest are they which do come into my presence for I am one sent of God the Father that they may be blest of me and by me - Such is my part - And for this have I walked with them - I have come unto thee that they may receive me - that they may come to know even as I know -

I say all which do give unto me credit for being that which I am - And unto their preparation due consideration and attention shall stand within my physical presence - They shall see me in tangible form. They shall counsel with me - and I shall give unto each his part -which has been prepared for him - I say he is now preparing himself for yet a greater part - For this have I given of myself - that they all be freed from their torment and bondage -

Were it not for thy benefactors ye should each remain in bondage - Yet we have volunteered to come unto thy rescue - And we have left our homes for thy sake - and as yet ye trouble thyself for such trifles - I say ye know not that which ye have forfeited I say ye have forfeited a goodly inheritance and I am come that ye may once again claim it - Such is my will for thee and I ask of thee prepare thyself for such as shall be given unto thee to do -

So be it that there are days near at hand which shall demand of thee all thy strength - all thy knowing - all thy wisdom and all thy attention So be it I shall be by thy side - And I shall sibor thee and I shall sustain thee. Yet ye shall be mindful of me and keep the law which I have given unto thee - So be it; it shall profit thee -

I am the Grand Worthy Master - Sanat Kumara

Sister Thedra of the Emerald Cross

Sanat Kumara speaking -

Beloved of my being - Blest art thou - and blest shall ye be - for I am come that ye may be blest - Was it not said that ye should be unto thyself true - Have I not said that there would be great trials and temptations and is it not so - Have I not said that ye shall not point a finger at another - Have I not said that there are none so foolish as them which think themself wise - Have I not given unto thee such laws as shall profit thee - I say ye shall study them well - And ye shall make them thy own and ye shall do well -

Be ye as one alert for I say the pitfalls are many - See that "ye" trip not - for too I say there's many a slip twixt the lip and the crystal goblet. I say "There's many a slip twixt the goblet and the lip" -

So be it ye shall make these laws thy own and forget that the other has tript should he -!

Ye have but the responsibility of thy own preparation - Such is thy own responsibility -

And it is now come when one shall walk among thee as one prepared for that which shall be done within this temple - I say one within this temple shall bring forth the new sibor which shall be as a new born baby fully conscious of his heritage and fully cognizant of his being -

I say this one which shall bring forth this child shall be as one prepared even as Mary - And which was Mary And which is Mary - which was the mother of Sananda and which is one and the same - I say unto thee: ye have given no thought unto these things and ye know not that which is - for ye see the appearance world - Ye see not beyond it - Yet I have said great things shall be revealed unto thee - I say be ye as ones prepared - for have I not said they shall come to know what is meant by the Virgin - And by the three wise men - So shall they and so be it and Selah --

Now be ye blest of me and by me for I am come that ye may be blest - Now I have commanded that the Seal be broken on the word which was brought back from the temple of the Andes and when it is brought out ye shall have proof of that which I now say unto thee - So be it and Selah -

I am thy older brother and thy Sibor - Sanat Kumara

Sister Thedra of the Emerald Cross

Sanat Kumara speaking to thee on certain things which shall profit thee to know - and to put into practice - I say unto thee that many has been sent into the earth even as our beloved brother and Master Sananda - for the purpose of bringing thee out of bondage - and I say unto thee it is the better part of wisdom to seek them out - And too I say as ye prepare thyself to receive them they shall reveal themselves unto thee - I say they reveal themself when ye are prepared for such revelation - Such is wisdom -

Too I say be ye not deceived by appearances for appearances are but the veil which stand between thee and reality - Be ye as ones which can see the beyond the veil - I am one which has been sent of the Father that ye may see - So be it when ye have sufficiently prepared thyself I shall personally come unto thee and sibor thee in the way of the wise - So be it for the good of all mankind - Amen and Selah -

Now I have given unto thee certain laws or commandments which ye shall follow - Put them into thy living - Make of them thy tools - thy handmaidens and it shall be unto thee thy key into the place wherein I am - And ye shall be received with great joy and much gladness -

I have said this is the testing ground - the proving ground - Let it prove thy worth - thy value for ones rebellious - full of wonton have no place within this temple - So be it all thy ways shall be directed in the way ye have set for thyself - Be ye not turned aside by appearance - or the opinions of others -

Bless them which sibor thee - Hear that which they have said unto thee - Be ye prepared for great revelations for they are being held for the time when ye are prepared to receive them - I say we stand with hands tied waiting for thy preparation - So be it a glad day when we can step forth as we really are and open up the records unto thee -

Blest shall ye be and glad shall we be - And let it be this day - Amen and Selah -

I am thy brother and thy Sibor - Sanat Kumara

Sister Thedra of the Emerald Cross

Sanat Kumara speaking -

Blest are they which come unto this altar -and blest shall they be - for I am come that they may be blest - for have I not set up this altar in the Father's name and have I not said that I shall be sufficient unto all thy needs - Have I not commanded of thee great things - Have I not said unto thee this is the proving ground - So it is -

I am not so foolish as to sibor fools - for I say I am not of a mind to give unto them of myself that they might give unto others that which be unto me my downfall - for I have received my inheritance and I am not of a mind to forfeit it - So be it ye shall be wise indeed to be unto thyself true and keep for thyself that which I give unto thee for thy own preparation - for it is for thy own sake that I now speak unto thee thusly for I say unto thee there are none so sad as the one which betrays himself or his trust - for I say they shall begin at the beginning and therein is the pity - So be as ones which know the law and for thy own sake I say ye shall abide by it - and let it be forever so -

Blest are they which come into the place wherein I am and I say unto thee it is now come when ye shall prove thyself worthy of such - for I say NOT ONE comes into this place unprepared for there are many keepers of the gates - And they know and know that they know - for they are not deceived by appearance -

When ye are given such as ye cannot bear - I say unto thee rejoice within your hearts for the trials which are but thy strength - I say thy strength shall be tested to the last - for this is thy preparation - I have said this is the proving ground - Will it not profit thee to prove thyself sufficient -

I say ye shall be unto thyself true and ye shall stand as the "Rock" and ye shall not be as the quicksand - and ye shall have within thy hand the sword of truth and justice and ye shall arise to any occasion - And ye shall be as one on whose shoulders rests the responsibility of thy own fortune - Ye shall not blame another for thy failure nor for thy fortune, for I say ye fortune unto thyself that which ye shall gather unto thyself. Such is the law -

Be ye as silent as the sphinx and wise as the serpent for therein is wisdom - Now too I say unto thee thou hast not yet begun thy work - This is only thy preparation and it is my part to bring unto this part - Yet ye shall put into practice that which I have given unto thee in the name of the Father Son and Holy Ghost - And ye shall be mindful of thy Source of being - And of thy benefactors and they shall remember thee in the day of thy trials - So be it and Selah -

I am thy Sibor and thy brother - Sanat Kumara

Sister Thedra of the Emerald Cross

Sanat Kumara speaking -

I shall add this unto the record which has been read at this altar - And it too shall be added for the benefit of all mankind - Let it be recorded as I give it - And not one word shall be changed for they shall bear witness of these my words and they shall see that which I have commanded thee to record -

I say I am the Grand Worthy Master of this temple which I have brought forth in the name of the Father Son and Holy Ghost - So be it I have come from out the silence that this may be brought forth for the good of all mankind -

I say ye which are so minded may come unto this altar for the purpose of hearing that which I say unto thee - yet I say woe unto any one which so ever casts one stone or which shall point a finger at the one which I have brot forth for the purpose of serving at this altar - I say I am as one accountable for this altar and I shall not allow it to be desecrated - for it is the law that when one sets his hand unto the priest within the temple he sets his hand against the sword of justice - Such is swift and it shall be done in the twinkling of an eye -

I am mindful of thy weakness and I shall warn thee aforehand - Be ye not so foolish as to trespass upon holy ground unprepared - Be ye as ones prepared and enter therein with joy within thy heart and be ye mindful of the Source of thy being - and of thy benefactors which have held thee fast in the hours of thy unknowing -

Bless them which sibor thee and be ye mindful of the Priestess within the temple - for I say unto thee she is my hand made manifest unto thee - Bless her and give unto her of thy love and of thy strength - Be ye blest for I am come that ye may have light - So be it and Selah -

I am thy older brother - Sanat Kumara

Sister Thedra of the Emerald Cross

Sananda speaking -

Beloved of my being I have called thee out of thy bed that this may be written - Even thru thy tears - I say unto thee it is time that they shall arouse themself from thy slumbers - I say they are asleep - I command of thee greatness in all things and I say unto thee arise unto thy station and command of them obedience unto the laws which I have caused to be written down - I give unto thee the authority to say unto them they shall arise and come forth from their sleep and they shall be as ones held accountable for thy tears - for I shall hold them accountable for their tears -

I say they shall arise from their slumbers and they shall put aside their puny ways - their small ego and they shall alert themself and they shall examine themself and they shall not point a finger at another for they have within their eyes no motes - Let their vision be clear - For first the mote shall be removed from their own eyes -

I say they dare not judge one another for the day of judgement is not theirs and they are not as ones prepared for it - Too I say each shall be his own judge and he shall be held accountable unto none other than himself - for there is none other to judge him -

I say when he has arrived within the inner temple he shall be wise and until then he has not the wisdom to judge - He has not the knowledge which is unto wisdom - I say he is the foolish one which holds his hand out unto the wind and says it is but a breeze which bloweth yonder and he knoweth not whence it cometh -

Beloved of my soul - Command of them justice - Command of them greatness in all their ways - I say unto thee be unto them that which I would have thee be - I say they are worse than asleep - They are dead on their feet - I say call them together in my name - Give unto them that which I give unto them - For their sake I have called thee out of thy bed - And I say unto thee I shall make of thee a pillar on which shall stand the light of the world - I say upon thy head shall rest a crown such as they have not seen - So be it and Selah -

I say ye shall call them together at evening time and at morning time and they shall be as ones alert and they shall give of themself and they shall give unto me credit for being that which I am - And I say I am a task master - For I demand obedience - and love one for the other.

I say again none shall point a finger at the other for he shall go within his was own heart and find therein that which he sees within his brothers and he shall find that which offends him within his own heart and pluck it out and he shall be unto himself true and he shall not excuse himself or cast it aside for another day - for he shall this day arise unto the occasion and cleanse his dwelling place - and purify himself -

For I say unto thee it is now come when ye shall stand as a rock - for the time grows short and ye have slept overtime and ye have given unto thyself credit for being wise when ye have been as the foolish virgins - Ye have had no wisdom - Ye have babbled as the foolish - ye have said things which has not been prompted by love - Ye have poisoned thy own cup - Ye have strewn thy own path with thorns which shall tear thy flesh -

I say I am not of a mind to see thee be devoured - And too I say I stand as one with hands tied - I am now prepared to lay heavy my hand upon thee and I would that I might spare thee for ye have not known me nor have ye heard me out - for I am not to be turned out nor am I to be cast aside - For ye have as yet not comprehended that which I am saying unto thee -

I have caused to be written many things and I say ye shall study these things which are written for they have been written for thee - for thy own salvation as part of thy preparation and I say when ye are in the temple thy attention shall be given unto the temple work and if it is given unto thee to be within the world of men then be unto thy trust true and be unto thy station true -

And go out from the temple as one of them and share with them their talents and thy darkness - Yet while ye are given the greater gift and the greater part why not be mindful of thy blessings - What sayest thou?

Be ye as one which has thy eyes folded over with many folds of dark cloth - thru which is no light seen - I say ye are blind as male moles Ye see not that which has been given unto thee - Ye ask not of the one which I have brought forth for the good of all mankind that this plan be brot into fruit - Ye are as ones walking in thy sleep - We thy Sibors call thee the living dead - We as yet have not reached thee - I say ye shall arise - Ye shall pick thyself up - And ye shall be as ones on whose shoulders rest thy own salvation -

And ye shall not be unto another a stumbling block - Ye shall be unto him a lamp - a living example of an initiate upon the path - And I have said when ye are so prepared I shall send one from out the inner temple which shall bring thee in and I shall be unto myself true - for I shall not fall asleep - as thou hast fallen -

I say I am about my Father's business and I am come that ye may awaken and if I have to put my foot against thy door I shall be sad indeed - but I have said again and again that none shall enter unprepared And I shall not deny that which I have said the law is the law and none are given preference - I demand for thee that which I am and I am one with the Father and I am obedient unto the law - unto every jot and tittle.

I command of thee awake and be about the Father's business - I say it is sad when one faints by the way or turns aside - for these are trying days - I say ye know not that which I say for ye are concerned with thy pettiness - thy own self will- I say ye are as little children playing with toys which ye shall tire of - Ye shall become weary of the petty things and ye shall call out for relief - Yet I say ye shall first be obedient unto the laws - for ye shall be as ones which have the will to be brought out of bondage -

And therein is thy deliverance - for none come unto thee for the purpose of entertaining thee - It is for thy own sake and we see thee as ones standing on the brink of destruction and ye know it not - I too say the hour swiftly approaches when ye shall be closed out - Or ye shall be closed in - in where nothing shall touch thee - for is it not written that there is a place prepared for thee wherein nothing shall touch thee in the day of sorrow - I say sorrow there shall be and it is near at hand.

While we thy Sibors sit at this council table that ye may become aware of that which we say at this table and of the plan which has been brought forth ye prattle as the parrots -

And ye know not that there are forces building up within the earth and about the earth which are accumulating at a great rate each and every moment - And it is written and wisely so that the moon shall go out as a wanderling - and the earth shall flip upon her axis - And I say unto thee ye sleep on and ye have not stirred in thy sleep - Pray unto thy God which has given unto thee thy being for the strength and the power that ye shall have need of -

I say all thy petty ways shall be as nothing - Ye shall stand face to face with thyself - Be as one loving and as one lifted up and be unto thyself true - For ye shall not say I have not spoken unto thee with my heart for I have cried out unto the Father with my being that ye may be brought before that day when the sun shall be turned into the bowl of blood and when they shall cry out in agony with the water and fire which shall mingle and which shall be unto them much torment -

I say the fire shall come up out of the oceans and the water shall rain down from the heavens mingled with fire - I say they, the elements shall be unchained and they shall not obey the command to be still - I say they shall not obey - for they shall no longer obey a drunken civilization - They shall no longer be comforted -

I say the earth shall no longer give footing unto a drunken people - And as for them which has been unto themselves true they shall be removed - Unto a new place of abode and they shall know no suffering and sorrow - for they shall be the ones chosen - for this shall they prepare themself -

I say they shall now give unto these my words their ear - They shall remember these my words for they shall be caused to remember them and they shall do well to read these words until they have come to know that which has been said -

I say unto them I have called my recorder out of her bed at an hour when they be sleeping that this paper be prepared for them and I say it shall be sent out unto all which have a mind to follow me - And too I say blest are they which do follow me for I am come that where I go they may go also - So be it the Fathers will - So be it - Amen and Selah

I am thy Sibor and thy brother - Sananda

Sister Thedra of the Emerald Cross

Sananda speaking -

I say unto thee which is my hand made manifest unto them - Ye shall now say unto them as I would say that they shall be as ones prepared for that which I have to say unto them and they shall have upon their own shoulders the responsibility of their preparation -

I say I can but point the way and they have to walk therein - And too I say that as a man prepares himself so he becomes -

Now for the first time I say unto thee I am the Priest within this temple and I have revealed myself for the purpose of giving unto thee light which shall be sufficient unto the day - And too I say ye shall be as one responsible and as ones grown to maturity - Ye shall be as ones responsible for all thy own offal - and for thy own reality and that which is real is not of the dream world - It is neither of the dead or the sleepers realm -

I say I am not among the dead - And I am not asleep - for it is given unto me to see and know that which goes on - And I am of the Father sent and I am within the place wherein all things are known and recorded -

I say unto thee I have within my hand the power to create like unto the Father and I say unto thee I am not a traitor for I know the law - And I say ye which are true unto thyself shall be as ones which shall have great revelation and ye shall first prove thyself worthy of such revelation - And ye shall be as ones prepared -

Ye have as yet not comprehended the word revelation and the word preparation for ye have not as yet had the proper preparation for such revelation as shall be given unto the just and prudent - So be it I would give unto thee my inheritance - And I would that I could bring thee in this hour, yet what would that profit thee - Ye should be as one kept out for lack of understanding of the law -

I have given unto the Father my word that I shall bring thee out of bondage and I am bound until ye have prepared thyself sufficiently that ye may be brot out - So be it I ask of thee prepare thyself for the day is neigh upon thee when ye shall either go out wherein I am and as I go or ye shall be as one turned back by thy own wonton and by thy own hand - So be it I shall be sad indeed -

I am thy older brother - Sananda -

Sister Thedra of the Emerald Cross

Sanat Kumara speaking -

Beloved of my being - Blest art thou and blest shall ye be - For I am come that ye may be blest -

Was it not written that ye shall be unto thyself true and give unto the temple work thy undivided attention? And I say unto thee it is in a deplorable state - Ye have given of thyself that ye may have the lesser part - Yet ye have not comprehended the fullness of thy work and ye have scattered thy energies - Ye have been but like unto children for ye hear and comprehend not -

I have said it is my part to give unto thee as ye are prepared to receive - And thy part to walk in the way I point unto thee - I say ye shall now alert thyself and give unto me credit for knowing that which I say - And knowing that which ye do not -

I say we give unto the Father all the credit and the glory - We are as Sons of God by our own efforts - For this have we worked - We have willed it so - So be it and Selah - Now ye shall say unto them in my name and as I would say - They shall be as one which has my hand upon them and they shall be unto themself true and they shall be as ones blest of me and by me - So be it and Selah -

Go from this altar with joy in thy heart and give unto the Father all the praise and the glory - So be it He shall remember thee - Amen - So be it -

I am thy Sibor and thy brother - Sanat Kumara -

Sister Thedra of the Emerald Cross

Sananda speaking -

Beloved of my being - blest are they which come unto this altar which the Father has set up - I say unto thee blest are they which come unto the source of all knowledge - and ask of God the Father that they may be learned of Him - And as they ask of Him He sends one of His own out that they may receive that which He has willed unto them - Now will it so that ye shall be brought into the place wherein I am and I say unto thee great shall be thy revelation and ye shall be glad for thy preparation -

Now let it be said that one shall come unto thee in the name of the Father Son and Holy Ghost - And he shall lead thee into the place wherein stands the great white altar of alabaster and ye shall stand before it and I shall declare for thee thy freedom - and ye shall be glad for thy preparation - Now be ye as one foretold for ye shall know the one which shall come unto thee - for it is written and wisely so that his countenance shall be so bright ye cannot look upon it - So be it and Selah -

Now was it not said that one should come unto thee and have I not said that he shall come in the name of the Father Son and Holy Ghost - I declare unto thee one shall come unto thee from out the inner temple and he shall be as none other for he shall have upon his head the Crown of the Sun and upon his forehead the Seal of Solomon - And ye shall know him for he shall be as none other - And I say ye shall be blest by him and of him -

Now be ye as ones prepared to receive him in the name of the Father Son and Holy Ghost - So shall there be much gladness and great joy - Blest are they which receive him - So be it and Selah -

Now let it be recorded that they which do go unto the white mountain on the day ahead shall be as ones blest for they shall be as ones which have my hand upon them and they shall prepare themself for that which shall be given unto them - I say ye shall go as one prepared to record that which I shall say unto them for I shall speak unto them and they shall heed that which I say - So be it. It shall profit them - I am with thee and I shall remember thee - So be it and Selah -

Blest art thou and blest shall they be which hear that which I say -

I am thy brother and thy Sibor Sananda

Sister Thedra of the Emerald Cross

Sanat Kumara speaking -

Beloved of my being - I am come that ye may receive of the Father as I have received and for this - shall ye be prepared - I say as ye prepare thyself so shall ye receive -

Too it is written and wisely so that none come into the place wherein I am unprepared - I say I AM - And I am within a place - I am not an imaginationary figure - I AM - And because the Father IS - I AM - And He has given unto me my inheritance in full - And I AM glad - I know such joy as ye know not of - I say for this is the way the Father has willed unto me - that I might come unto thee that ye might be brought out of thy bondage - in love mercy and in wisdom -

I say it is the better part of wisdom to receive us - in love and with an open heart - than the wandering which ye have chosen -

I say of thy own free will have ye gone into darkness - And of my own free will have I given of myself that ye may be brought out -

Now I would give unto thee this day this word - When ye are properly prepared I shall step forth and as one in flesh and bone and I shall touch thee with my hand which ye shall be able to feel and touch as even ye can touch any other - And I shall call forth the elements and I shall command of them to obey thee - And this shall be done in the presence of one which is known unto us as Sananda -

I say unto thee these laws are not revealed unto the unjust or to the IMPRUDENT - for we are not so foolish as to betray ourself - for we have been diligent in our part -- and I say I have spoken unto thee in wisdom and with love - I am a merciful man - I am of the Father sent that ye may receive thy freedom from all bondage -

Be ye as one which has the mind to comprehend that which I say and it shall profit thee - I ask of thee pray for thy memory - Wherein is stored all knowledge for therein is wisdom -

I say thy memory is sealed up and too I say it shall be broken and I am glad - I say ye shall pray for thy memory and ye shall receive and have I not said "I shall stand before the great white altar within this mountain and declare for thee thy freedom - So be it and Selah -

I am thy Sibor and thy brother - Sanat Kumara

Sister Thedra of the Emerald Cross

Sanat Kumsra speaking

Blest are they which come to this altar and blest shall they be --And I say unto thee ye shall be as ones which have my hand upon thee for great is the need for them which have the will to serve within the plan which has been brought forth for this new day and - for this new dispensation - Yet I say unto thee ye have dragged thy leg irons with thee from past ages and they have been unto thee great weight and have held thee within thy tracks bound I say ye have not been freed - as yet from thy bondage - Yet let it be said again that we thy Sibors of the Royal Assembly have come that ye may be freed - I SAY AGAIN AND AGAIN YE HAVE NOT KNOWN THE MEANING OF FREEDOM I say ye are in bondage - Ye are bound by such laws as ye have fortuned unto thyself And ye have been in darkness for lo many eons - Ye have not remembered thy inheritance willed unto thee of the Father

Now I say it is come when ye which have the will to remember shall be quickened and ye shall give unto me credit for knowing that which I say - Ye shall be quickened and ye shall remember all things Ye shall know even as we know for it is the Father's will - I say He is a generous Father - He is merciful And He has willed unto thee His vast estate - He has willed unto us <u>You</u> and <u>Me</u> all that He has All that He is - And be ye as one prepared to receive it -

Now I say ye shall prepare thyself for such as He has willed unto thee And He has gone the long way with thee for He has waited long for thy return - I say ye have gone out from Him and to Him shall ye return -

Blest are they which do return for they shall go into darkness no more - And I say they shall know no sorrow - I say they shall receive their own godhood

Blest am I for I have received my inheritance in full - And I come unto thee that ye may receive of the Father as I have received - So be it every man's inheritance -

I am now prepared to come unto thee - And to give unto thee as I have received of them which have gone before me - And when ye are so prepared I shall come unto thee as one in tangible form and I shall give unto thee a part which is strange and new unto thee, And I say I shall reveal many things unto thee - So be it that ye shall be glad for thy preparation Be ye blest even as I am blest -

I am thy Sibor and thy elder brother - Sanat Kumara -

Thedra of the Emerald Cross

Be ye as one blest of me for I have seen thee within the place wherein ye are as one which has a mind to learn - And now I say unto thee ye shall be as one which has my hand upon thee and ye shall say unto them in my name that they shall be as one man for they shall have need of their strength and they shall be as ones which have the responsibility of their own preparation - And I say that they shall be as "<u>One</u>" for in unity there is strength - And I say ye shall stand as one man - for therein is wisdom -

And it is now come when there shall be one among thee which shall be as one sent out from the den of the dragon - And that one shall deny me for that one shall be as none other - For it is given unto that one to serve the forces of darkness - And to serve the fallen one - When ye have joined thy self together as one man under the banner of truth and justice not one shall prevail against thee for I say in unity is strength

Now were it not so dark within the earth we, thy Sibors and Benefactors should wait for yet another day when the efforts of the illumined ones would be of less strain - I say it would be the easier part Yet there is a great necessity to bring forth the martyred saints and the illumined ones from other realms that there might be enough light within the earth that sufficient balance may be brought about to keep the earth on her course and for this do we work at this time -

I say we have worked diligently that the earth and the children thereof may be delivered out of darkness - Out of bondage - I say unto thee - Love ye one another and ye shall be blest of me and by me - And let it suffice that I am thy older brother and call me the Nameless One - So let it be.

I am one sent of God the Father - I come from out the silence - So shall I speak again and again - So be it and Selah - Blessings forever more

Sister Thedra of the Emerald Cross

One of Sananda's best maxims:

"It has been said the tongue is the devil's best weapon - Why not disarm him?"

Sanat Kumara Speaking -

Blest art thou and blest shall ye be- Ye shall this day go into solitude with thy "---" and ye shall be given a part which has been prepared for thee and ye shall wait for a time wherein ye shall be blest of Me and ye shall be as one- for I say ye shall go into solitude within the place wherein the last part was given- for another part shall be given as that one- When it is done the one which has given the place shall be called and likewise the one which is now absent- I say the one which is now absent shall sit with thee in the place of seclusion- and too I say, while ye are gone from this temple wherein ye are- it shall be prepared for thy return and that which ye have received shall be given unto them- So be it it shall profit them -

Now I say ye shall go straight way within the hour and ye shall be as one obedient to the command and ye shall wait for a time for thy blessing -

I say go straight way within the hour and ye shall go from this altar in silence into that place and with thee shall go the one on thy right side- He too shall go in silence-

I am with thee and I shall be with thee to the end-.

Blest art thou and blest are they which gather about this altar which has been brought forth thru the Great White Star- Allejua - Allejua -

****

Be ye at peace and blest shall ye be- and seek ye the light of the Christ for ye shall be as one on whose shoulders rests great responsibility -

And it is now come when one among thee shall be given a part which shall be new and which shall be unto him a great responsibility- for in the time which is near he shall be brot before the great white altar for the purpose of gaining wisdom- I say he shall be brot before the great white altar for the purpose of gaining wisdom and there shall be a place for him in which he shall serve as one which has been prepared-

And now when ye have called them together ye shall read this my testimony unto them and they shall remember these my words and they shall be as ones which have the will to hear that which I say unto them- So be it: it shall profit them-

For the first time I say unto thee one shall go out from among thee as one prepared- for a new part- and that one shall stand before the great white altar within the holy mountain wherein ye are and he shall be as one prepared for the greater part- So be it and Selah-

I am now come that he shall be alerted and prepared- So be it and Selah-

With my own hand I shall bless him---.

I am thy older brother Sananda

Sister Thedra of the Emerald Cross

Sanat Kumara speaking

Beloved which has come unto the altar of Gods which have within them the fortune willed unto them of our Father- which is every man's inheritance- I say it is every man's inheritance to be a Son of God- A God within his own divinity and so let it by the grace and love of the Father which has given unto us being- So be it- Amen and Selah-

I say unto thee ye have gone out from the Father as one perfect- and unto Him shall ye return perfect even as ye went out- yet ye shall be as one which have prepared thyself for thy return-.

I say unto thee ye have had thy memory blanked from thee- and it is now come when ye shall will that it be restored unto thee- and if and when ye ask of the Father that it be restored one shall be sent unto thee for the purpose of being unto thee his hand made manifest and ye shall be glad to receive Him and to receive of Him for He shall declare for thee thy freedom-

So be it: it shall profit thee to ask of the Father thy freedom and again I say He shall hear thee- and ye shall not be turned away- and He shall receive thee unto Himself with much gladness and great joy such as ye have not known- Blest are they which do return unto the Father- for they shall receive of Him their Godhood- Such is thy inheritance- Such is the Fathers love and mercy and ye shall profit by thy preparation- I say ye shall be blest for I am come that ye may be blest-

Now I say unto thee at this altar that one shall come unto thee and he shall direct thee and ye shall be as one prepared to receive him- Now let it be recorded thusly-

Ye shall receive one at this altar which shall be sent from out the great white mountain wherein stands the altar of white alabaster- and he shall be unto thee much light and give unto thee great revelation- for I say ye shall be unto thyself true and ye shall be prepared to receive Him and He shall know thee as ye are- He will not be deceived for He has been well trained for this part- Now be ye as ones which have my hand upon thee and I shall bless thee and I shall follow after the first

one- Such is my preparation for I have become that for which I have prepared myself - And I have received my inheritance in full-

So Be it and Selah- I Am thy older brother and thy Sibor-

Sanat Kumara

Thedra of the Emerald Cross

Father-Mother God – Benefactors – I, Thedra come to this altar which you have set up – for the good of all mankind – Let it be known unto me this day how I can better serve thee and the plan you have brought forth. I bring myself as a living sacrifice. Use me as you will. Glorify thyself in me – and through me, and cause me to walk in the Light of the Christ forever and forever.. So be it as thou hast willed it.

Sananda speaking –

Beloved of my being I say unto thee this morning as I have given unto thee so shall ye give unto them – I say ye shall give unto them which are of a mind to receive that which I have given unto thee for them – that they may have light –

And is it not written and wisely so that I am now in the earth prepared to reveal myself unto them which are prepared to receive me and of me – I say they which do give unto me credit for being that which I am and for being the Son of God – Sent as such and fortuned to be the one which comes in His name – for the purpose of bringing unto the earth Light – which is thy deliverance from all bondage – Then and only then shall I reveal myself unto them –

I speak unto them which sit within the places of darkness wherein they are bound – Wherein they serve the forces of darkness – I say they which labor for bread shall see that which binds them and that which has been unto them the millstone about their neck – I say they shall see that which has been unto them their leg irons and they shall be as ones which have a mind to turn from it and to seek the light –

They shall flee from that which has bound them and they shall call for the light – for knowledge of their being – They shall seek the light which is eternal and wherein all things are known – Wherein is no mystery – I say that which has mystified thee shall no longer be a mystery – for all things shall be revealed unto them which purifies I and are found worthy and prudent –

I say we thy Sibors are not so foolish as to sibor traitors and fools, for therein would we be betraying our trust and ourself –

Blest are they which are found worthy - I am come that ye may have light – yet I say ye shall prepare thyself for such revelation as shall profit thee – So be it and Selah-

I am one sent of God the Father and he which was once called Jesus of Nazareth –

Now known in the Temple of Light as Sananda –

Sister Thedra of the Emerald Cross

Sanat Kumara speaking:

Blest are they which come unto this altar in the name of the most high living God - I say they shall be blest of Him and by Him - Blest are they which have received my words and which abide by that which has been given unto them - As the part which shall be unto them their preparation - I say blest are they which prepare themself for the greater part - I say they shall walk and talk with me - And they which walk with me shall see God face to face - So be it and Selah -

I say this is the greater part - And for this has He-the Father sent me unto thee that I may bring thee out of darkness - Such is my part - And it is thy part to prepare thyself for the greater part --

Now I ask for thy freedom - I declare for thee thy freedom -

Now have ye been as diligent - Have ye willed it so -

Have ye watched thy tongue - thy every thought -

Have ye been in the place of the publicans -

Have ye floundered to shallow waters -

Have ye slept on thy feet -

Have ye remembered what has been said in this house of God - At this altar -

Have ye given unto my hand made manifest the credit due -

Have ye waited by the wayside for the thief which would pick thy pocket and slap thy face -

Have ye been watchful of thy own way - How can ye sleep upon thy feet?

I say ye as yet have not applied the laws which have been given unto thee - And too I say be ye not dismayed for the sincerity of purpose is a great treasure to be held within thy heart - And none shall take that from thee - And too have I not said I see thee as ye are and not as ye appear to be - I say there is a law which I am one with that shall be revealed in this age - And for this do I claim for thee thy freedom - And while it is yet time I ask of thee let no words pass from thy lips which would bind thee - for each word is that which would free thee - or bind thee - I say ye know not the power of the spoken word - Be as a guardian of them - for as the fouls of the air they return unto their resting places. And great shall be the joy thereof - or the stench - Be ye not so foolish as to dung thy place of abode - I have said: "Unto the waters I dung - I purify" -

Blest are they which have ears to hear - Let him hear - And let him be the one to cleanse himself and receive of the water of life - So be it he shall go into darkness no more - Amen and Selah - Sanat Kumara

Sister Thedra of the Emerald Cross

Be ye blest of my presence and of my being -

I say unto thee I am with thee and I say I am, for the Father has sent me unto thee that ye may have thy inheritance which He has willed unto thee - Now my children I say unto thee as He the Father would say - There are none so sad as he which would betray himself and too I say there are none to bind thee against thy will -

I say ye shall not be bound against thy will - And too I say ye have will all thy woe - And sorrow - And it is now come when ye shall will for thyself the greater things - I say ye shall be as ones which have reached the age of maturity and ye shall walk as men and ye shall not be afraid - For I say no man shall decree for thee thy bondage - for I have come that ye be brought out of bondage - And I say unto thee I am not of a mind to come into the places wherein the porcupines dwell I say I am not so foolish for I go not into the den of the porcupines for they are not prepared to receive me -

Now I say unto thee ye shall rest at peace and be ye at poise for I am saying unto thee that they know not when they say ye are surrounded by the porcupines - Be ye not deceived - Nor be ye afraid - Have I not given thee my word I should go before thee that nothing evil or of darkness should overtake thee - I am not asleep nor am I in lethargy - So be it my patience are strained - So be it my love exceeds my patience - So be it ye shall try my patience again and again yet I shall bear with thee a while longer - Yet ye shall not mock me -

I am thy Sibor and thy brother - Sananda

Sister Thedra of the Emerald Cross

Excerpts -

"Give unto me credit for being that which I am - and give unto me credit for knowing that which I say unto thee - And I shall give unto thee the part which I have kept for thee."

Sananda

Sanat Kumara speaking -

Beloved of my being - Blest art thou for I have lifted thee up - I have brought thee into the place wherein I am - And I have given unto thee a portion which ye have sealed up and which shall be opened for all to see and know at a later time when they have been prepared for such a portion - I say it shall be revealed unto them - And too I say no man <u>can</u> pilfer such knowledge - It has been written and recorded for thee that they shall not eat of this tree of Knowledge - I say ye get not such knowledge by the food of thy mouth - Ye get not such knowledge by the reading of such books as ye have acquired -

Ye have not such knowledge available unto the unjust and the imprudent - I say ye do not acquire such knowledge as is revealed through the source of thy being - And it is the law when ye acquire such knowledge it is by and thru revelation - I say revelation is a gift of God the Father willed unto thee as part of thy inheritance - And ye shall now give unto the Father credit for thy being and unto thy benefactors credit for that which they are and unto them credit for thy well being - And unto thyself credit for being a Son of God -

And love thyself and ye shall be as one blest of the Father Son and Holy Ghost - Amen - So be it and Selah -

Go thy way this day rejoicing that it is now come that ye shall have within thy hand the POWER to receive that which has been willed unto thee and I say that power shall be revealed unto thee in the name of the Father Son and Holy Ghost - It has been written and wisely so that no man climbs up any other way - And so it is - And so be it - that any man which pilfers such knowledge is a thief and shall not enter into the kingdom of God - So be it that ye shall come by the way set before thee

I am come that ye may be brought in - in love, harmony and in dignity I say ye shall return unto the place of thy going out in dignity - So be it and Selah -

I am thy elder brother -

Sanat Kumara -

Sister Thedra of the Emerald Cross öz

Excerpts......

"Love thy life which is endowed unto thee of the Father - and thy freedom is assured thee."

From the Sibors teachings

Through Thedra

Sanat Kumara speaking -

Blest art thou and blest are they - I say ye shall be blest of me and by me - for I come that ye may be blest   So be it and Selah -

Now for the first time I say unto thee ye shall have none of the misery which is fortuned unto them - for I shall be unto thee a shield and a buckler -

Be ye as one prepared for that which I shall give unto thee to do - for in the time which is near I shall call upon thee for a part which is new and strange unto thee and ye shall respond in haste - Such is obedience and such is wisdom -

Now let it be said that ye have been obedient in all things and ye have answered every call - and with my own hand have I directed thee Now I shall give unto thee a part which shall prepare thee that ye may lead them even as I have led thee - And it has now come when they too shall step forth and take up the yoke and be as ones which can assume such responsibilities as goes with such an ordination - for it is the times which has been prophesied when every man shall stand and as one, fight shoulder to shoulder or he shall perish as with a great blast from out the north - I say as with a great blast from out the north -

Ye have as yet no concept of my words and their meaning - Yet I say as one shall ye stand or perish - For within the world of man are many which have the will to overcome all thy good works and all thy knowing - I say they are the agents of the fallen one and they shall be put down - And too I say ye are as the emissaries of light and it is required of thee this day to hold the Light of the Christ in balance - that even the elements shall obey thy loving command - And I say unto thee Watch every word which proceeds from thy mouth - And ye have gone a long way when ye have mastered thy tongue - So be it a battle won -

I am now with thee for the purpose of giving unto thee that which shall profit thee - And ye shall either accept it or reject it - And blest are they which shall use it for their own sake -

I am thy older brother and thy Sibor - Sanat Kumara

Sister Thedra of the Emerald Cross

Sanat Kumara speaking -

Be ye blest of my presence and I say unto thee ye shall be as ones which have my hand upon thee - And ye shall walk upon thy feet as man - for it is now come when ye shall be brot out of darkness and ye shall will it so - So shall it be - I say ye shall will it so. And so be it -

Now let this be recorded this day - that I shall take from this place one which I have brought in - And too I say ye shall be as ones which have gone the long way that this may be accomplished - Ye shall wonder at these my words yet ye shall have them at thy finger tips - for ye shall be caused to remember them -

Now ye shall refer to thy Bible for the purpose of reminding thyself that there are times when things are given unto thee aforehand which ye do not comprehend at the time --- I say ye are prepared aforehand - So be it the better part of wisdom -

I am now prepared to give unto thee the greater part - Ye shall prepare thyself to receive it -

I am thy Sibor and thy older brother - Sanat Kumara

Sister Thedra of the Emerald Cross

* * * * * * * * *

Sanat Kumara speaking -

Beloved of my being be ye blest of my presence - and of my being for I am come that ye may be blest - So be it in the name of the Most High Living God - Amen - So be it I am in the place wherein I shall declare for thee thy freedom and I say unto thee there are none within this place which are not prepared for the part which they have -

And too I say that there are fourteen within this place wherein stands the great white altar of alabaster and wherein stands the priest which is our beloved brother Sananda - I say we have gathered ourself within this place for the purpose of giving unto certain ones a part for which they have waited - I say that there are three within this place this day which are now being prepared for their ascension - I say that we have been brought into this place for the purpose of giving assistance unto these brothers -

And too I say it is not new unto us for we are about the Father's business - And we are not unaware of our part and of the inheritance willed unto us of the Father - So be it that I am now prepared to bring thee in and to give unto thee as we have received - So be it and Selah -

I say ye shall now give unto them this part and they shall hear from my own lips that which I say and as it is plainly written and well recorded that they may have knowledge of such - as they have not known - I say they shall come to know such that which goes on within the realm of light -

Now I say unto thee some shall be filled with opinions - Some shall say Nay! Nay! And so shall it be - As they are prepared - for I say unto thee there are none so foolish as the one which thinks himself wise and none so sad as he which betrays himself - So be ye as wise as the serpent and silent as the sphinx - I say boast not of thy knowledge - for ye have not as yet heard or seen that which ye shall see or hear - I say ye shall come to know that which has been hidden from thee - So be it and Selah

I am with thee and I shall be with thee unto the end - So be it and Selah -

I am thy Sibor and thy brother - Sanat Kumara

Sister Thedra of the Emerald Cross

Sanat Kumara, speaking -

Beloved of my being blest art thou - and blest are they which come unto this altar which the Father has set up - So be it in His name - Amen and Selah -

Now it is come when ye have gone out and to Him the Father shall ye return- I say ye shall return unto Him even as ye went out - Perfect as in the beginning -

For the first time I say unto thee ye have this day earned the right to call thyself a Son of God the Father for ye have been given thy inheritance in full - Yet ye have not accepted it and for this shall ye prepare thyself - For it is now come when many shall come unto thee for the purpose of gaining wisdom - And I say ye shall be as one prepared for thy new part which has been prepared for thee - And I say unto thee as ye prepare thyself so shall ye receive - And this is the law: As a man prepares himself so shall he become -

Now it is given unto me to see them running to and fro looking about them for the solution of all their woes - Yet they find no solution for they look in the places of darkness - And therein is no wisdom - I say they have not sought the source of their being nor have they asked of the source - I say they go about within the world of men as ones lost They know not whither they goest - Neither do they remember their source of being - And therein is the pity - Blest are they which seek their source - And blest shall they be -

I am come that ye may have thy inheritance given unto thee in full. I say ye shall accept it in the name of the Father Son and Holy Ghost. Amen and Selah -

For the first time I say one shall come unto thee with his credentials within his hand for he shall carry within his hand a goblet - A crystal goblet of which I have spoken many times - And I say when ye see that goblet within his hand ye shall ask that ye may drink and I say when ye do drink of the water from the crystal goblet - Ye shall step forth from the dense form of physical substance into the body of light substance which shall be thy Whole body - thy Holy body - the Christ body - which shall not bind thee -

And ye shall be free from the gravitation of the earth and free from the attraction of the moon - Such is thy inheritance and even more I say ye shall return unto them as one prepared to lift the dead - heal the sick and to cast out demons - Such shall be part of thy part - Such is he which has received the greater part - Blest is he which has the greater part for he shall have within his hand all power - And he shall be one with it - He shall be trustworthy in all things - He shall have the power to create like unto the Father - And he shall have the wisdom which is given of the Father - Such is the Father's will - So be it and Selah -

I am thy older brother and thy Sibor - Sanat Kumara

Sister Thedra of the Emerald Cross

Sanat Kumara speaking-

Blest are they which come to this altar and blest shall they be-

Now let it be recorded that as a man prepareth himself so shall he become- I say he becomes that for which he prepares himself- No man cometh into the place wherein I am unprepared- So be it and Selah-.

Be ye as one which has my hand upon thee and I shall lead thee into the place wherein I am- And I shall bless thee as I have been blest- So be it ye shall receive even as I have received- of God the Father - So be it- Amen and Selah-.

Blest are they which do receive as I have received- And blest shall they be- And it is my part to prepare thee to receive as I have received- Yet ye shall do thy part and ye shall walk in the way set before thee- Such is thy preparation- And when ye are so prepared I shall come unto thee and consul thee even as I am- And have I not said that I shall come into the world of flesh even as ye are- of flesh and bone shall I come- and I shall sup with thee and I shall speak unto thee in words which ye can hear and comprehend- And ye shall know as I know- for I shall cause thee to comprehend-

I am prepared for such an occasion- And I am not so foolish as to Sibor fools and traitors- I say I do not Sibor the foolish for I am not of them and they are not of Me- for they have not prepared themself to receive Me - So be it I shall keep my word and I have said it- So be it- Amen and Selah-.

I am thy Sibor and thy older brother- Sanat Kumara

****

Sananda speaking-

Blest are they which come unto this altar which the Father has set up- and I say unto thee He has willed for thee a place wherein ye shall be brought in the time which is near- And I say ye have as yet not begun thy work for as yet ye have not prepared thyself for the greater part- Yet it is time that ye be prepared-.

And I say that one shall present himself unto thee when ye are prepared to receive Him- And too I say ye shall present thyself at this altar in a befitting manner and ye shall give unto Me thy undivided attention and ye shall be reminded of thy shortcomings- for they are many- And I shall remind thee again and again- I say ye shall come unto this altar in a befitting manner and ye shall prepare thyself aforehand and come as ye would should ye enter into the citadels of the world-

I say ye have been as ones which have not the mind of the elite and ye have been lax in thy ways- Ye have been thoughtless of Me and My presence-.

Be ye as ones respectful of thy benefactors and of thy own self for I am with thee and I demand respect in all things- so be ye as ones reminded- So be it I shall speak unto thee again on this subject-.

I Am thy older brother and thy Sibor- Sananda

Sister Thedra of the Emerald Cross

Sanat Kumara speaking:

Blest art thou and blest are they which come onto this altar which has come into manifestation in the name of the Father Son and Holy Ghost - So be it that all which do come shall be blest - Amen and Selah

I am now prepared to bring thee into the place wherein I am and to give unto thee as I have received - So be it that I have received my inheritance in full - Amen and Selah -

Be ye as one which can comprehend the laws which have been set before thee and abide by them - And ye have but to walk in the way set before thee -

I say walk ye in the way set before thee and ye shall profit thereby. Blest are they which abide by laws given unto them - And too I say ye have been given a new dispensation and a new law - for ye are now privileged to come the easy and safer way - for many have come into the earth that ye may have help; that ye may be brought out in this day And too I say ye are no longer of the old order -

Ye are under a new law - And a new dispensation has been given unto thee and ye have as yet not comprehended that which is being done that ye may have thy freedom while it is yet time - For the great day draweth near when there shall be great torment and great sorrow - for within the earth and about the earth is great source of darkness which shall come forth into manifestation; and I say that it is NECESSARY that ye get into the proper place wherein ye are to work within the plan and then when ye have been assigned thy place -

Ye shall give unto it thy whole time without exception and with joy and with dignity - And I say it shall be an example to all people - For within these places - I say within these temples which shall be set up we do give explicit instructions which are for thy own good and for the good of all mankind - I say we are not so foolish as to betray ourself or our trust - And I say if the sibet should turn aside that another shall be brought out to fill his place - Yet pity shall he be which does turn aside.-

I am now come that this plan shall be fulfilled - So shall it be - Amen and Selah - My Father has entrusted unto me this part and I have come voluntarily - And I shall see it through unto the end - Such is my word unto thee - I am of the Order of Melchizedek - which I have spoken of and I say unto thee ye are of the Order of Melchizedek and of the Order of Sarah - And there are certain brothers which shall guard and be unto thee shields from the world - And I say they shall be called the "Sons of Sarah" - for they have been given the Seal of Sarah and they shall carry with them a seal which shall be given unto them -

And they shall be aware at all times of their sacred responsibility - And too I say it is a most sacred responsibility and it is given unto me to know; and woe unto any man which defiles his sister for he has upon his heart a seal - And that seal shall be broken and he shall see himself as he is - And he shall know that which is - which was - and which shall be - I say he shall be as one come alive and he shall know that all things are his and he shall not transgress one law - without paying so dearly - poor in spirit is he which transgresses a law knowingly - And pity is he which knows not - for he is in darkness

Blest is he which is brought out of darkness - And his reward shall be great indeed - Blest am I to be privileged to come unto thee - So be it I am glad - I am thy older brother and thy Sibor-

Temple of Sananda-Sanat Kumara

Sananda speaking unto thee at this hour -

There are ones from the realms of light gathered together at the altar within the heart of the great white mountain wherein stands the white altar of alabaster -which do come together for the good of all mankind. And so be it: it is in the name of the most high living God -

Now I have said unto thee that one shall stand before this altar and declare for thee thy freedom - I say that one now stands within this place wherein there are ones from three temples which have come from out the realms of light - They come that the law might be filled - that the earth may give up her secrets - that the ones so prepared may be brought in and given the part which has been kept for them -

Now I say that there are many from the world of men which shall be found and brought out from them which shall be brot in and given a new part and which shall go out again as ones prepared for a new part And I say ye shall be given as ye are prepared to receive -

Now let it be said ye have come into this place - even within this building wherein ye are for the purpose of serving within this plan which is now unfolding before thee - And I say ye have not yet begun thy great work which is yet to be revealed unto thee - I say as yet the greater part has not been revealed unto thee -

I too say that when ye are prepared ye shall receive even as I have received and ye shall be glad for thy preparation -

I have said this is the path of initiation - So it is and so be it in the name of the Father Son and Holy Ghost - Amen and Selah -

I am within this place prepared to bring thee in and to give unto thee a part which is yet to be revealed unto thee and I say there are none so foolish as he which thinks himself wise and none so sad as he which betrays himself or his trust -

Be ye as ones true unto thyself and I shall bring thee into the place wherein we now sit in council for thy own benefit - I say we have received our inheritance in full - Yet ye have forfeited thy own - So shall ye have it returned unto thee as ye are prepared -

Now for the first time I say unto thee that one in this place has come from a far and distant galaxy wherein is no darkness - And for this holy event and on this occasion which is new unto thee have they been sent of the Father that there may be a close tie or bond between that planet or galaxy and that of thy own - I say that this is the occasion for great joy and much rejoicing -

Too I say ye have not as yet learned the secrets of the initiate which ye shall come to know- and for this do ye prepare thyself-.

Too it is said and wisely so that none find their way into this place with measuring rod and tape- and neither do they come unprepared- for they have to have the proper credentials- And I say we are not fools or traitors- for we know thee even as ye are and I say ye shall come clean of hands and of heart- for ye have but to cleanse thyself of all thy lusts- all thy rebelliousness (wonton)- and of all thy hatreds- all thy jealousy- all thy pettiness and forever free thyself of thy own legirons which ye drag after thee- and I say from this day forward shall we watch thee as one which has presented thyself for admittance within this temple-.

And as I have said unto thee many times "Unto the waters I dung I purify"- So be it the better part of wisdom-.

I am thy older brother and thy Sibor- Sananda

****

Be ye blest of me and by me- and be ye as one upon which I lay my hand and I shall lift thee up and I shall bless thee- and I come unto thee that ye may be blest- For it is now come when ye shall go out into all the lands of the earth and ye shall touch them and ye shall heal them of all manner of infirmities- And for this are ye being prepared- So be it I am with thee and I shall not forsake thee for I forsake not my own- I am within the place wherein I am prepared to come unto thee and to give unto thee a part which is new unto thee and ye shall be as one prepared to receive it- So be it and Selah-

I say unto thee they shall be blest of Me and by Me- Such is my word unto thee- Amen- So be it and so shall it be- Let it be-.

I have spoken and my word shall not return unto Me void-

I Am Sananda-

Sister Thedra of the Emerald Cross

Sanat Kumara speaking -

Blest art thou and blest are they which come unto this altar which the Father has set up - for they shall be blest of Him - for it is now come when they shall be brought out from among them and they shall find within themself that for which they have sought -

I say they have run hither and yon looking for that - which they know not and they have found no peace - Now it is come when peace shall be established within them - for I say we, thy Sibors have come that there might be peace - I say we bring not peace - Yet we make way for peace - Blest are they which do find it -

Now when ye are so prepared one shall come unto thee and he shall touch thee and ye shall know the peace which is his, and ye shall be blest of him, and by him - Such is his part to come unto thee and open up thy memory - And ye shall know as he knows - Ye shall remember thy being - and thy time before ye went into darkness - Ye shall remember thy being which was before thy going out from the Father - thy day before going into bondage -

Ye shall know that which is meant by freedom and love - Ye shall know the law governing all things - and ye shall be free forever more - And ye shall go into bondage no more - Such is his part - And it is thy part to prepare thyself to receive him - And I say unto thee he is not a fool - for he has the fortune to know thee as ye are - and he goes not out on a fools mission nor does he be deceived by appearances -

I am now prepared to receive them into the place wherein I am when they are prepared to come - Wherein I am are fourteen - And when they are prepared for to be brought in - this place shall be ablaze with the lights which shall come in, for it is the plan that when the next one is brought in, that a sign shall appear within the sky and they shall see it from afar - And I say unto thee ye shall prepare thyself for ye may be given a sign which ye have not seen and which ye know not - Yet ye shall remember these my words and ye shall be alert - for many strange things shall come about in the time which is near-

And I say unto thee which do read these words - Be ye not opinionated for thy opinions shall be as the dew before the noon day sun -

Blest are they which turn unto their Source of being for all knowledge - for they shall come to know even as I know and I have received my inheritance in full -

I am a Son of God the Father - known within the inner temple as the Ancient of Days - Called the Worthy Grand Master - Sanat Kumara

Sister Thedra of the Emerald Cros

Sananda speaking:

Be ye blest of my being and of my presence - for I now come unto thee that ye may come unto me and that ye may know me as I know thee - So be it in the name of the most high living God - So be it and Selah -

Will ye not know me as I know thee? Have I not said that I shall give unto thee as ye are prepared to receive? And is it not the law? I say ye shall first prepare thyself to receive me - and have I not sent my emissary out before me? And have ye accepted her? Have ye given unto her credit for being that which she is?

And have ye given unto her credit for being that which she is? (This was repeated in the message) I say as ye receive one of my emissaries ye have received me - And too I say as ye set foot against one of them ye have set foot against me - for I send my emissaries out in my name and as ye are prepared to receive them I send them unto thee - And as ye put thy hand to their mouth - so do you seal my lips. And as I have said many times - When ye give unto one of my prophets the bitter cup - ye give it also unto me - And when ye have gone the last mile ye shall know whereof I speak - Such shall be thy knowledge -

I am now prepared to reveal many things unto thee which are prepared for such revelation - Now I am saying unto thee such things as shall profit thee to remember - And remember them ye shall - for it is now come when ye either go forward or move into another place - for I say unto thee that the earth shall no longer give unto the sleepers comfort and she shall no longer mother an ungrateful civilization - an ungrateful people - for she shall vomit them out - and spew them up - for she is weary of them.

And I say the elements shall no longer obey the willful and wonton people which have thought themself wise - Too I say that there are none so foolish as the one which thinks himself wise and none so sad as he which betrays himself or his trust - So be it that he shall be confronted with his foolishness - And he shall be brought to account for his foolishness - So be it and Selah -

Now when I say I am within the secret place with many of my brothers from the realms of light, I am speaking literally and truthfully for I am not a liar - and no man shall prove me a liar - For I am not to be found wanting -

I have said I am within the earth in a garment of flesh and bone - and I have come unto this one which now records these my words unto thee and I have ordained her for this part as one qualified to speak unto thee for me - for I say she has been prepared for this part and sent forth to do that which I have commanded of her - So be it I say again - Woe unto any one whoseoever sets hand upon her - And I say she shall be unto herself true - for I have sibored her wisely and I say the things she will not say - So be it I shall speak that which I am of a mind to - and no man shall stay me or set his hand to my mouth -

And I am He which is sent of the Father for the purpose of bringing thee out of darkness - So be it-It shall profit thee to hear me out - I have spoken - Have ye heard me? I shall continue to speak and it shall profit thee to hear - I am He which was born of Mary and which was the ward of Joseph - Once called Jesus of Nazareth, now known in this temple as Sananda Son of God - Amen So be it and Selah -

Sister Thedra of the Emerald Cross

Sanat Kumara speaking:

Beloved of my being - Blest art thou - and blest are they which come unto this altar in the name of the Father Son and Holy Ghost - So be it and Selah -

While it is still time I shall give unto thee this part which shall go out unto them which shall be prepared for the greater part - And I say unto them that there are places within the earth which has been prepared for this day and wherein man has not set foot - Ye think thyself wise - Yet ye know not that such places do exist and let it go on record that these places are held in trust by the Hierarchy and is the inheritance of them which are fortuned to be part of the new dispensation -

This is the work of the new dispensation and it is given unto me, Sanat Kumara, to be the one responsible for this part of the work - I have volunteered for this part, and I have given of my love and of my wisdom of myself that this age may bear fruit -

So shall it - Amen and Selah -

Blest are all which do accept that which has been held in trust for him - I say unto him - He is no longer bound by the old law; he is under a new law and he has been given a new dispensation whereby he may come into his inheritance in this day - and whereby he may have his leg irons cut away - *

Now I say here for thy benefit that there are none so foolish as he which thinks himself wise and none so sad as he which betrays himself or his trust.

And it is given unto me to see thee seeking hither and yon for relief from all thy woes -

Yet ye have not turned unto the source of thy being and ye have not asked of God the Father thy deliverance -

I say unto thee in His name - When ye seek thy deliverance in Him and thru Him - He will send one of His emissaries unto thee and as ye receive him He shall send yet another - A Son of God - And I say unto thee ye shall not be deceived, for there shall be given unto thee comprehension of these things -

I say unto thee - Pray for comprehension and seek the Light of the Christ and all that is necessary shall be revealed unto thee - So be it and Selah -

Now for the first time I speak unto thee on the subject - Wherein I am are many which have come from other realms - from out thy solar system have they come - And they are of the Father sent - Even as I am sent -

And with thy Lord and Master which ye have called Jesus of Nazareth and which we call Sananda - sits one from out thy own system wherein there is only light - No darkness exists there - And he has come that his light may be added unto ours - And he is of great stature -

For he stands fourteen feet tall by thy standards - And we herein this temple know him as Bearea, for he has been unto thy solar system a mentor and a guardian - We have asked of him that he may be unto us a lamp when thy earth has seemed to go out of sight - for her blackness has been great - She has had little light - And her darkness has been great indeed - Be ye mindful of them which have gone out from their place of abode for thy sake -

Now this brother Bearea, shall make himself known in the world of men - For he has great power within him - for it is given unto him to be one with the Father that this may be accomplished in due time - And when he speaks it shall profit thee to hear him - for he shall reveal great knowledge - Such is his part -

I am within this place wherein I am host unto him - And we herein sit at this council table for the good of all mankind - And we are thy benefactors which do guard and keep watch that thy earth and the children thereof do not go into perdition - Such is our mission - And it is thy part to hear that which we say unto thee and to prepare thyself to receive the greater part - Which is thy inheritance in full - So be it and Selah.

I am thy benefactor and thy older brother Sanat Kumara

Sister Thedra of the Emerald Cross

Sanat Kumara speaking:

Blest art thou and blest are they which come unto this altar which the Father has set up - So be it that many shall come thru these portals and I say unto thee - all which do come shall be blest and so shall they come to know that which is willed unto them of God the Father - And they shall receive of Him their inheritance - So be it His will - Amen and Selah -

I am within the place wherein I sit in council for the good of them which shall be brought in - And blest shall they be, for they shall have upon their head a crown and upon their forehead the Seal of Solomon.

I say that in the time which is near many from among the populace shall be brought into the place wherein there is a great white altar of alabaster and they shall be fortuned that which has been held in trust for them -

Now I say unto thee ye shall be as one prepared - for none enter into this place unprepared - for it is the Father's altar and none shall desecrate it - I say we are not so foolish as to give unto fools our pearls without price - We are not traitors nor do we give without the consent of the Father for He has given unto us with wisdom and within the law. And we abide by such law as He has fortuned unto us - We are not bound by it - for we are one with it - Yet we transgress it <u>NOT</u> - Neither do we tempt the Father which has given unto us free will - Such is wisdom.

I say we are within this place as ones prepared for this day - And we have set up quarters within this place within the great white mountain wherein the white altar of alabaster now stands - And with us is one from another solar system which ye shall come to know and ye shall be as ones given a great privilege to be blest of him and by him - I am now prepared to give unto him the place of honor wherein he shall give unto thee his part and his blessings shall follow thee - So be it and Selah -

I am thy brother and thy Sibor Sanat Kumara -

Bearea speaking:

Be ye blest of me and by me - For this do I reveal myself unto thee My beloved sister of the Emerald Cross it is only a short while since I last spoke unto thee in the high Andes - And at that time ye knew not that ye should return into thy homeland for this part - And that I should come into the earth for this my part - I say it is the will of the Father that we work within this place for a time and that which is to be done shall be accomplished according to a great and divine plan which has been brot forth from the inner temple - fashioned of the "one" and thru the love and mercy of our beloved brother Sanat Kumara - Known as the Most Worthy Grand Master - has this plan come forth - I say the fullness of this plan shall be revealed unto them which shall be brought in - Such is the Father's will - So be it and Selah -

Now I shall speak with thee on the morrow and I am glad - So be it ye shall go from this altar in peace and with dignity and I shall remember thee in the hours of thy sleep - Amen, So be it in the name of the Most High Living God and Selah -

I am thy elder brother Bearea -

Sister Thedra of the Emerald Cross

Sananda speaking:

Blest are they which come unto this altar and blest shall they be - For they shall come to know that which has been hidden from them -

I say blest are they which keep thy lights bright and they shall be made Keepers of the Flame - So be it that this day I shall speak with thee on the subject of <u>ONENESS</u> and for this do I come unto thee - Be ye as one prepared to receive me and of me and I shall give unto thee a part which ye shall give unto them which are yet in bondage -

Now from the beginning of thy going out from the Father in to the world of darkness have ye been one with Him in reality - Yet ye have separated thyself from Him in thy own mind - And in thy own UNKNOWING ye have forgotten thy identity and thy Oneness - For ye have not remembered Him - the Source of thy being or the fortune willed unto thee of Him the Father -

And ye have been as ones soul-less, for ye have wandered as ones without direction - As ones lost in the wilderness - Knowing not whither nor whence - And ye have now reached a place wherein ye have no other place to turn - Ye have no other way to go and ye have been as one which have fortuned unto thyself all thy woes and torment.

Ye have NO OTHER to blame - Ye have NO OTHER to account to – Ye shall be either the victor or the loser -

It is now come when great shall be thy woe and so great shall be thy sorrow that ye shall fall upon thy face and cry aloud for mercy - I say ye shall turn unto the Father, the Source of thy being for mercy and ye shall put aside all thy pettiness and all thy puny ways - for it shall be unto thee thy own salvation -

Now hear me in this - I say let no man cause thee to turn aside from thy appointed course - Ye shall hold firm unto the course set before thee -

Ye shall be unto thyself true and give unto no man the bitter cup - for woe unto him which gives unto his brother the bitter cup -

I am within the earth for the purpose of bringing unto thee light and I am not to be turned aside - So be it and Selah -

I am thy Sibor and thy brother Sananda -

Sister Thedra of the Emerald Cross

Sanat Kumara speaking -

Beloved of my being be ye blest of me and of my presence for I now come unto thee that ye may be blest - I now bring unto thee for them this part - which shall be given unto thee for them - And by thy grace shall ye receive it for them -

Be ye prepared to receive the blessed and beloved from out thy own solar system which we know as Bearea - And for this has he come that the way may be made clear that there might be free communication between this realm and thine - I say there shall be ones prepared to receive him and of him for he comes unto us as one qualified for his part which is given unto him of the Father of us all - So be it and Selah.

I am one which has stood sponsor for thee and I have sibored thee and wisely so - Now ye shall record for them that which he has for them, and be ye as his hand made manifest unto them - So shall ye be blest - Amen and Selah - I am Sanat Kumara -

Bearea

Blest art thou among woman and blest shall ye be - for I come that ye be blest - and I speak for the ones which now sit within this council chamber with me - That as ye come unto this altar which has been brought into manifestation we, thy Sibors and thy brothers of light draw neigh unto thee and we do breath the breath of life upon thee - I say we do breathe the breath of life upon thee - And as yet ye know not that which does sustain thee and hold thee fast -

I say we, thy Sibors from the realms of light do hold thee fast in the hours of thy unknowing and I say ye shall come to know us - For we have left our places of abode and come into thy place wherein ye labor for bread - that ye be delivered from bondage - I say we have gone out from our place of abode for thy benefit -

For we have not gone into darkness for our own benefit - We need no such lessons - for we know wherein ye are bound - and by what ye are bound -

And forever has it been: Wherein is darkness is no light - I say wherein is darkness is no light - And be ye as ones which have a will to turn unto the light and seek the light of the Christ and one shall come unto thee in the name of the most high living God - which shall be unto thee his hand made manifest unto thee - And he shall touch thee and ye shall be as one come alive - And ye shall see him and know even as we see and know - And ye shall drink from the crystal goblet the living water - And I say all which drink of the water of life shall not die for death shall have no power over them and they shall be free, forever free as we, thy Sibors are free -

I say unto thee we are not bound by any law - for we are one with all law and we are true unto our station - We walk upright and with dignity - We forget not our inheritance which is willed unto us of the Father which has given unto us being -

Now for the first time I come into thy own earth and I find here in many which are prepared to receive me and of me - And for this I am glad - And from the beginning of my going out from my place of abode have I sent unto them my love and my wisdom and I have spoken unto them in the hours of their sleep that they might be prepared to receive me - and of me -

Let it be entered into this record that I have not spoken through another from the beginning have I prepared this sister of the Emerald Cross for this part - And too, I say I shall use no other channel - Yet let it be known that these fellow brothers of light do use many and shall use any and all which are so prepared - I say never within the history of man has it been so necessary that there be kindled within thy hearts the flame of love - One for the other -

I say ye shall pray without ceasing for love such as ye have not known - for the day draweth near when ye shall turn unto thy Source of being for light and for mercy - And let it be said here - When ye do call out for mercy with thy heart black with hate ye shall be as ones cast out - For I say ye shall be as ones cast out of thy own foulness -

Blest are they which turn unto their Source and ask for light and which do come clean of heart and hands -

Such is my word unto thee - And I shall speak unto thee again and again - Be ye at Peace this day and be ye Poised - And I shall remember thee -

I am thy older brother and thy Sibor - Bearea -

Sister Thedra of the Emerald Cross

Bearea speaking:

Blest are they which come to this altar - And blest shall they be - for they shall come to know that which has been unto them their blessing -

I am come unto thee that they may come to know that which has hitherto been hidden from them and ye shall be unto them my hand made manifest unto them- And for this do I now give unto thee the authority and the power to speak in my name -

And say unto them as I would say - that when they have prepared themself they shall have the gift of communication and the gift of speech - the gift of hearing and the gift of sight - for these are but parts of thy inheritance and as yet - they have but partial sight - and hearing and they use their gift of speech to defile themself and to desecrate the temples - for they are blasphemous and they say not that which is prompted by love - And that which is given unto them of God the Father They say that which binds them - They are as ones bound by their own wonton and by the darkness fortuned unto the unknowing ones - Such is the pity -

Now give unto them this word - When they use these gifts which are the lesser ones for the glory of God the Father - they shall be added in great measure and they shall see and know - even as we, thy Sibors, see and know - I say we see and know without limitation, for we are not bound by any limitation - We are free -

Blessed are they which are free - And I say we, thy Sibors have come from out the silence that ye may be free - And I say unto thee, forever clean thy heart of any and all hatred - all malice - And give unto the Father God- all the glory and all the credit - And give unto thyself credit for being a Son of God - And take unto thyself the responsibility of thy own self and the part which has been given unto thee - Carry thy load with joy and thanksgiving - and call no man thy tormentor - for ye are alone responsible for all thy torment - Ye alone are responsible!

Say unto thyself: He is not my salvation or my tormentor - He is my brother - Unknowingly or knowingly - I say ye shall take from him the power to torment thee -

Ye shall be so filled with joy and love that he <u>SHALL</u> see thy light and thereby light the lamp -

Such is my word unto them - I say ye shall remember these my words - And when ye have learned them well I shall give unto thee greater things which ye have not dreamed of - And great shall be thy reward -

I say no man enters into the place of the most high living God unprepared - And I have come that ye may be prepared - So be it: it shall behoove thee to prepare thyself - And all the keys are contained within these my words - And have ye found them? Ye have but to seek within thy own temple for the light which never fails and that which burns upon the altar of the most high living God -

Now within a short while one shall walk within the world of men as one fully qualified to give unto thee the water of life - And I say ye shall drink thereof and pass from thy dense form into thy Holy Christ body as one purified and as one cleansed from all darkness - and death shall be no sting - for death shall have no power over thee -

Ye shall ascend unto the Father even as thy beloved brother Sananda, the Lord and Master, which ye have known as Jesus the Christ. I say within the record that many have ascended - for this is the day when these things shall become common knowledge unto every man - And they shall know that which has been hidden from him - Such is wisdom -

I say revelation is a gift given unto thee of God the Father and willed unto thee as part of thy inheritance - So be it ye shall prepare thyself for such revelation - Such shall profit thee -

I speak unto thee from out the secret place of the temple of light wherein sits the council of many lights and I say they are within the earth for the purpose of giving unto thee as ye are prepared to receive - No more - No less -

Ye have been told and warned of such as shall come upon thee and ye have not heard - Ye have gone to sleep on thy feet - And again and again the word has gone out from all the temples of light - Prepare thyself for the Great Day is near - When the sun will give unto thee no light - And when ye shall be given much torment OR - Ye shall be removed into a place wherein is no danger NOR NO darkness - I say ye have been warned - And yet ye sleep -

I say - Yea ye are as the walking dead and ye shall be as ones which do seek the light - Or ye shall GO OUT in deep sleep - And I say woe unto him which does go out in deep sleep - for he is the ones which have betrayed themself - I say there are none so sad as the one which betrays himself or his trust - Blest are they which turn their face homeward - For one shall be sent unto him and he shall receive that for which he has prepared himself -

Keep ever before thee these my words and I shall remember thee -

I am thy older brother and thy Sibor -

Bearea - of the

Sister Thedra of the Emerald Cross

Sananda speaking:

Beloved of my being - Blest art thou my beloved - For this have I revealed myself unto thee and ye shall come into the fullness of thy inheritance this day - So be it the Fathers will - And I am glad - Amen and Selah - Ye shall give this unto them and they shall bear witness of these my words - So shall it profit them -

I say unto them that they shall have proof of me and I shall give unto the worthy proof - Yet I shall not satisfy their curiosity nor shall they pilfer my secrets nor shall I betray my trust - For I am of the Father sent that His will be done in me - thru me - and by me - And I do not betray myself or my trust - For I know the ones which are prepared to receive me and of me -

I am not so foolish as to sibor fools - or give unto babes my pearls without price - Too I say that there are ones which have slept over-time and they shall be caused to awaken - And they shall be as ones come alive and they shall arise and come forth and they shall be glad their sleep has ended - For they shall be as ones awakened from a long and troubled sleep wherein they have dreamed dreams which have tormented them -

I am glad this day is come - For I say unto thee there are many which shall come forth from out the populace which shall be unveiled and they shall stand forth in all their glory - For they shall be as ones which have the Crown of the Sun upon their heads and the Seal of Solomon upon their forehead -

I say that they now walk among thee unknown - And uncrowned - Yet I say they shall be unveiled - And they shall become known in the world of men - even as they are known unto us - I say be ye alert for ye shall walk with angels unaware - For this do I now speak unto thee that ye may look for thy own light which burns upon thy own altar - within the temple of the most high living God - And then ye shall see and know that which is now hidden from thee -

First ye shall be true unto thy own self and unto no man give the bitter cup - Such is wisdom - Now I say unto thee - Ye shall follow the law which is set down for thee and ye shall be blest - for thy own sake do I remind thee of thy short comings - And I know thy weakness - And too, I know wherein thy strength lies - Such is my knowing -

I say unto thee I am He which ye have called thy brother Jesus of Nazareth - born of Mary and the ward of Joseph - Now known within the place wherein I am as Sananda Son of God - So be it - So let it be - Amen and Selah - I have spoken unto my hand made manifest unto thee known within this place wherein I am as Sister Thedra of the Emerald Cross - So be it she shall be blest of me and by me and as I have willed it so be it - Amen and Selah -

Sister Thedra of the Emerald Cross

Sananda speaking:

Be loved of my being - Blest art thou and blest shell ye be for I am now come that ye may be blest - For none shall place before thee a stumbling block - And none shall set his hand unto thy mouth -

Now let it be said that there shall be one which shall come unto thee from out of the place wherein I am and he shall instruct thee in the procedure which ye shall follow - And this has been given unto the one which shall come from the great council of the White Star - Or the White Brotherhood - As ye so frequently put it - It is lawful to speak thusly -

Now ye have asked of us help of a practical type - And of that which shall be unto thee practical within thy own realms - Such is lawful - for there is no need to give unto them which are not prepared to receive that which should choke them - I say we give not the babe at the breast the flesh of animals - Such is wisdom - I say when they have come to the age of responsibility they shall be given accordingly - Such is wisdom -

Now was it not said in the beginning that one should come unto thee - And I say again one shall come unto thee from out the place wherein I am and he shall counsel thee and he shall give unto thee instructions in the way in which ye shall proceed within this temple - And he shall be unto thee great light and he shall be as none other - For he has been within this place for many moons - And he has not gone out -

And I say unto them - Be ye not opinionated for ye shall be found wanting - And there is none so foolish as he which thinks himself wise So be it and Selah - I am with thee and I am glad - Such is my part to come unto thee that this plan may be fulfilled - And so shall it -

I am thy Sibor and thy brother Sananda -

Sister Thedra of the Emerald Cross

Bearea speaking -

Blest art thou among women and blest shall ye be: I am come that ye may be blest - So be it in the name of the most high living God - Amen and Selah -

By my own hand shall ye be blest - for I say unto thee I have come into the earth from a far and distant galaxy that this age might bear fruit of a new kind - And within the time which is near - nearer than ye can imagine - one shall be born of woman - From the womb of woman shall he be born and he shall come into the world of men as one sent of God the Father and he shall be from out the realm which I call my own - I come as the forerunner - I come that the world may be prepared to receive him -

Now let this be recorded for them that they have not seen - or heard of this one which shall come - for he has not been born of women - He is of the Father sent that this age may bear fruit of a new kind - I say he is leaving his place of abode for the first time - He has as yet not come unto the earth as man - Nor has he taken a body of flesh upon any other planet within thy own solar system - For the first he shall be embodied within the world and never at any time has he been born of woman -

So be it that this shall be for the first time - And I say ye shall be within the body of flesh when he is born of woman - of the woman shall he be born -

Give unto them these my words and say unto them as I would say that they shall put within the records these words which bear witness of these things which are yet to come - And by thy hand shall these words be recorded for them - And blest shall ye be - for ye know not that which ye shall do. And I say ye have yet not begun the greater part.

Give unto them this word - and they shall remember them - At the age of twelve years this one shall make his entrance within the world of men - And then I say unto them he shall set up a temple upon a hill and he shall call forth the maxim light and it shall burn upon the top of this temple which shall be seen far and wide - It shall beckon them from afar and they shall come unto this temple of which I speak - which shall be builded upon the hill - And therein they shall be prepared for their ascension -

And I say they shall no longer be the ones which die and rot within their graves - They shall transmute all the elements of earthly substance and take them with them into the realms of light from whence they came -

They shall speak the "Word" and the elements shall obey their command - And they shall be thy hand maidens in joy - and in thanksgiving - They shall be unto thee that which ye will - Such is my word unto thee - I have spoken unto thee from out the secret place wherein sit the council of light that they may come to some knowledge of these things. So shall it profit them - Amen and Selah

I am thy Sibor and thy older brother from yet another solar system.-

Bearea -

Sister Thedra of the Emerald Cross

Temple was held at sunrise this morning on Holy Ground on the mountain.

Sanat Kumara speaking unto thee that they may know that which is now established - I say unto thee that they may know these things which shall be revealed unto thee.

Now when ye have been prepared for this part ye shall be taken into the heart of this mountain wherein stands the white altar of alabaster -

And I say unto thee ye shall say unto them as I would say that there are none so foolish as the one which thinks himself wise - and none so sad as the one which betrays himself or his trust -

When there is sufficient light within thee - ye shall be brot into this place wherein there sits the Council of Seven Lights - And I say unto thee the Council is now in session - I say the Council sits within the place wherein the altar of white alabaster now stands - And on that altar now lays the words which were written at thy fireside on the night of July - when ye did stand upon this Holy ground - I say the words which were written now lay upon this altar -

And where upon sits the Sananda-Sanat Kumara symbol which shall be read as follows for the first shall I give it unto thee ---- This symbol is not to be given out as such - For it is not to be made known unto the world of men -

I say ye shall read this unto them and they shall be as one which shall ask to see it - yet ye shall guard it for the future work - It shall be unto them their proof - And none shall pilfer it - this symbol -

I am thy Sibor and thy brother - Sanat Kumara -

Sanat Kumara speaking -

Blest of my being - Blest art thou among women and blest shall ye be - So be it and Selah - I say unto thee ye shall be blest for I now stand ready to come unto thee and to give unto thee that for which ye have waited - Such is my part with thee - And I say I am not bound by the flesh as thou art -

Now ye shall have upon thy forehead a seal and upon thy hand a shining thing which is not of this world - For I say ye shall go out from the place wherein ye are as one prepared - So be it and Selah -

Blest art thy partner for he has given unto thee richness of heart unknowingly - I say he has served thee well - While not knowing -

Now will it so that ye may be brot out -

I am thy Sibor and thy brother - Sanat Kumara -

Sister Thedra of the Emerald Cross

Sanat Kumara speaking:

Be ye blest of me and by me - for I am come that ye be blest - I say unto thee ye shall be blest of me and of this council - Ye shall be blest of all which do sit with me - For within the place wherein I am are many which have come from out the realms of light that ye may be blest - Have I not said that there is one among us at this time which is from a distant galaxy wherein there is no darkness - And if it were not so I would not tell thee -

Now he shall speak with thee and ye shall give it unto them which are of this temple - And blest shall they be -

I say not one shall misuse his words nor shall they say they are NOT SO - for I say unto them - Woe unto any man which desecrates them - for this one is sent even as I am sent of the Father - And I say the law is swift indeed and it shall rebound upon them - I say there are none so foolish as he which betrays himself - And one which has within his mouth profanity shall surely reap the results thereof

Blest art thou that he has come unto thee - I say ye have prepared thyself for to receive him and of him -

Bearea

Be ye as one which has my hand upon thee and I shall bless thee O my child - And be ye so blest of me that ye may be unto them that which I am unto thee - I say ye have been blest - so ye may bless others in turn. Go into all the lands of the earth and bless them -

I say it is near when ye shall go out and ye shall go into the land of Egypt and into the dark continent of Africa - Wherein there is much torment - Wherein there is no peace - And ye shall give unto them that for which they have waited -- They have waited such light as ye shall carry - Ye shall then go out as one free from all bondage - free forever.

I say ye shall have free concourse into all the lands of the earth and into all the nations of the earth - I say ye shall be unto them great light and much strength - Ye shall counsel the heads of such governments as shall reign supreme - I say that the heads of all the governments shall ask for thy counsel - for they shall be as ones bewildered and confused. And they shall be glad for thy light -

I say ye shall go unto them in the name of the most high living God as one prepared and as one sent as an emissary of God the Father - I say the Father God has so willed it and none shall deny Him nor shall they take away from Him - He shall bring about the fullness of this plan which has been brought forth for the good of all mankind - So be it and Selah -

I have spoken unto thee my recorder and ye shall give it unto them in my name and they shall bear witness of me - and that which I have said unto thee for they shall come to know such things and it shall profit them-

It is said that there shall be many brought out from the populace and they shall be prepared that they too shall go out for the good of all mankind- I say that there shall be brot into this council chamber ones which are so prepared and they shall be so instructed that they may serve in this plan in such capacity- and blest shall they be- For their reward shall be great indeed-.

I have spoken that they too may know that which goes on within the realms of light- Amen-So be it-.

I bless thee with my being and with thy hand have ye recorded my words unto thee- And ye shall sign thyself unto this document and unto all documents- for they shall go on record and they shall become part of the permanent records now kept at Lake Titicaca- Such is my word with and unto thee this day-

I am thy brother and thy Sibor Bearea--.

****

Beloved ones- I say unto thee this day- one shall come unto thee and he shall be unto thee as one which has my hand upon him- He shall be as one which has gone out from the place wherein I am and he shall be blest of me and by me and he shall be as one which has upon his head a crown-- and upon his forehead a star-.

I say unto thee he shall come unto thee as one prepared for that which shall be given unto him to do- I say he shall come as one prepared-

Now ye shall prepare thyself to receive him and ye shall be as ones which have thyself in order- For I say he cometh in the name of the most high living God- So be it ye shall receive him in such manner as is befitting a brother-.

I am with thee and I shall bless thee- So be it and Selah-

I am Sanat Kumara

Temple was held at sunrise this morning on Holy Ground on the mountain.

Sanat Kumara speaking unto thee that they may know that which is now established - I say unto thee that they may know these things which shall be revealed unto thee.

Now when ye have been prepared for this part ye shall be taken into the heart of this mountain wherein stands the white altar of alabaster -

And I say unto thee ye shall say unto them as I would say that there are none so foolish as the one which thinks himself wise - and none so sad as the one which betrays himself or his trust -

When there is sufficient light within thee - ye shall be brot into this place wherein there sits the Council of Seven Lights - And I say unto thee the Council is now in session -

I say the Council sits within the place wherein the altar of white alabaster now stands - And on that altar now lays the words which were written at thy fireside on the night of July - when ye did stand upon this Holy ground -

I say the words which were written now lay upon this altar - And where upon sits the Sananda-Sanat Kumara symbol which shall be read as follows for the first shall I give it unto thee ---- This symbol is not to be given out as such - For it is not to be made known unto the world of men -

I say ye shall read this unto them and they shall be as one which shall ask to see it - yet ye shall guard it for the future work - It shall be unto them their proof - And none shall pilfer it - this symbol -

I am thy Sibor and thy brother - Sanat Kumara -

Sanat Kumara speaking -

Blest of my being - Blest art thou among women and blest shall ye be - So be it and Selah - I say unto thee ye shall be blest for I now stand ready to come unto thee and to give unto thee that for which ye have waited - Such is my part with thee - And I say I am not bound by the flesh as thou art -

Now ye shall have upon thy forehead a seal and upon thy hand a shining thing which is not of this world - For I say ye shall go out from the place wherein ye are as one prepared - So be it and Selah -

Blest art thy partner for he has given unto thee richness of heart unknowingly - I say he has served thee well - While not knowing -

Now will it so that ye may be brot out -

I am thy Sibor and thy brother - Sanat Kumara -

Sister Thedra of the Emerald Cross

THE SEAL

Sanat Kumara speaking-

Blest of my being - Blest art thou among women and blest shall ye be - So be it and Salah - I say unto you ye shall be blest for I now stand ready to come unto thee and to give unto thee that for which ye have waited - Such is my part with thee - And I say I am not bound by the flesh as thou art -

Now ye shall have upon thy forehead a seal and upon thy hand a shining thing which is not of this world - For I say ye shall go out from the place wherein ye are as one prepared - So be it and Selah -

Blest art thy partner for He has given unto thee richness of heart unknowingly - I say He has served thee well without knowing -

Now will it so that ye may be brot out -

I am thy Sibor and thy Brother - Sanat Kumara -

****

The Crystal Goblet
The Poseid

Beloved of my being - Be ye blest of Me and My presence -For this have I come - I say unto thee ye shall now receive that for which ye have waited - Be ye blest of the presence of one which we know as The Poseid and be ye as one which has His hand upon thee and He shall bless thee and give unto thee that which shall prepare thee for thy part.

I say ye shall now record that which He has for thee and it shall be for the good of all mankind - So be it and Selah - I am with thee and I shall stand sponsor for thee - I AM - and I AM - for thy sake I am come unto thee that they may receive this and for their sake do ye receive it for them which are of a mind to receive the greater part - Amen and Selah -

The Poseid speaking -

Blest are they which receive Me and of Me - For I now come unto thee as one prepared - that ye may give unto them as ye do receive of Us from out of the realms of Light - I say ye shall receive of Us and as ye do receive ye shall likewise do unto them which are so prepared - I say as they are prepared so shall they receive - And so let it be -

I say unto them that when they have sufficiently clean

Sanat Kumara speaking:

Beloved of my being - Be ye blest of me and of my presence - For this have I come - I say unto thee ye shall now receive that for which ye have waited - Be ye blest of the presence of one which we know as the Poseid and be ye as one which has his hand upon thee and he shall bless thee and give unto thee that which shall prepare thee for thy part.

I say ye shall now record that which he has for thee and it shall be for the good of all mankind - So be it and Selah - I am with thee and I shall stand sponsor for thee - I AM - and I AM - for thy sake I am come unto thee that they may receive this and for their sake do ye receive it for them which are of a mind to receive the greater part - Amen and Selah -

The Posied speaking:

Blest are they which receive me and of me - for I now come unto thee as one prepared - that ye may give unto them as ye do receive of us from out the realms of light - I say ye shall receive of us and as ye do receive ye shall likewise do unto them which are so prepared - I say as they are prepared so shall they receive - And so let it be -

I say unto them that when they have sufficiently cleansed their dwelling place that they shall receive yet another wherein they shall dwell within the realms of light wherein is no darkness - And for this have we, thy Sibors which are not of the earth and which are no part of darkness - come unto thee that ye may be delivered out -

I say when ye have delivered thyself out - And when ye have come out from among them which are yet in bondage - and them which do serve the dragon - one shall come unto thee and give unto thee as ye are prepared to receive -

Such is our part - I say we are of the Father sent - And we give not our pearls of price to babes which know not their worth -

I say we do know their worth and we do sibor thee wisely and we do come when ye are ready to receive of us - and by us - It has been said many times one shall come unto thee bearing a gift more precious than frankincense and myrrh and so shall it be - I say again it is with the greatest of love and mercy that this one shall come when ye are prepared to receive him -

He shall bear upon his forehead the Crown of the Sun - He shall have within his hand a crystal goblet - beautiful beyond compare - And he shall have within the goblet the water of life - from which all things perfect are made and which makes perfect all which it touches -

I say it purifies and cleanses all which it touches - And anyone which so ever drinks of this liquid of life shall not die - They shall step forth from their body of earthly substance into their body of light substance as one delivered from all bondage - And from all darkness - And their leg irons shall be cut away - Forever free shall he be - So be it that their deliverance shall be unto them their crown and their robe of light - The seamless garment - And it shall enfold many which ye shall deliver up - So be it and Selah -

Now I say unto thee "---" while it is yet time ye shall be as ones true unto thyself and prepare thyself - for ye shall be called in the midnight hour - And ye shall hear that call and ye shall answer it and ye shall be glad indeed when ye are prepared to receive the cup bearer - I say ye shall be glad indeed - Such is my word unto thee -

I am thy older brother and thy benefactor - The Posied

(Leg irons - Karma)

Sanat Kumara speaking -

I say unto thee - my own - As I have not said before - I now stand ready to bring unto thee one which stands with thee - which shall be unto thee thy shield and thy buckler and I say unto thee ye shall be as one which has my hand upon thee - And I say ye shall be as one which has given of thyself that they may be blest -

Now ye shall give shelter unto he which is to come and he which shall be unto thee a hand and a foot - And I shall be unto him all that is necessary for he shall come unto thee as a brother and he shall be as one which has a mind to serve the Christ - And he shall be as one sent of God the Father - And he shall stand by thee as one which has the will to serve the light -

I say he shall serve the light with all his strength and I say ye shall have cause for rejoicing - So let it be - Amen and Selah -

I am now prepared to bring him unto thee - So be it that he is now prepared - And I am glad - So be it ye shall receive him in the name of the Father Son and Holy Ghost - Amen and Selah -

I am Sanat Kumara

Sister Thedra of the Emerald Cross

Sanat Kumara speaking unto thee - I say ye have gathered thyself into this temple for the purpose of learning the greater things - I say as ye are prepared so shall ye receive -

Now again I say unto thee - Ye shall be given as ye are prepared and I have said that none enter into this place wherein I am unprepared And too I say that when one is so prepared that he has done well and such is wisdom - I say that none shall come into this place save through the open door - And too I say I am the Grand Worthy Master - And I am guardian of the secrets which are held in trust for them which are found worthy and which do abide by such laws as is given unto the initiate upon the path or the candidate for such initiations as shall make him eligible to enter into this temple -

I say when he has properly prepared himself one shall come unto him and say unto him - My child I have watched thy goings and thy comings - And I find thee worthy that ye may now be received into the place wherein I am going - Ye shall now pass this way - And I say unto thee that which is wise and prudent - Yet ye shall NOT be sufficiently learned to pass these portals by saying that which I have said unto thee for I am not so foolish as to give my pearls unto babes who know not their worth -

I say ye shall earn thy passport into all the secret places of the earth. And too I say by thy works ye shall be known and all thy good words shall avail the nothing lest thy motives shall be clean - pure of heart and clean of hand shall ye present thyself - I say again - All thy words of sweetness shall avail thee naught - when ye have within thy heart one iota of selfishness - and one dark place within thy heart -

I say cleanse thy own heart and come clean of heart and hand and one shall come unto thee and he shall lead thee out - And I shall meet thee at the door wherein I am and I shall ask of thee three questions - and when ye can answer these truthfully ye may enter - and until then ye shall remain outside - while ye shall be as one in darkness and know not the workings of the temple -

Now I say unto thee - Inasmuch as ye are faithful in little things - ye shall be made keeper of greater - I say ye shall be given in greater capacity and in abundance - I say all law shall be revealed unto the just and the prudent which do enter into this temple wherein sit the Council of Seven Lights - I say we are the lights of this temple - I say we are the guardians of thy earth and the welfare thereof - I say ye shall come to know of this council and the workings thereof - I say ye which are prepared to enter herein shall be schooled in the ways of the wise - And therein is wisdom - So be it part of thy inheritance - So be it the will of the Father -

I have spoken - So let it be as I have spoken - And I have come unto thee that they may know that which I have said - Such are my words and give them unto them which are prepared to receive them - for none other shall receive them - Such is their misery - They are deaf and blind and I am not of a mind to give unto them sight and hearing until they ask that it be given unto them - When they will it so - so be it - And it shall be as they will -

I am he which guards this temple door - I am Sanat Kumara -

Sister Thedra of the Emerald Cross

Sanat Kumara speaking unto thee at this altar this day - Beloved ones I say that none are excluded from this temple - Yet not all are prepared for this part - And when they shall find their way - And were it not so there would be no need for this my part of 'this plan' -

Be ye as one on whose shoulders rest great responsibility for within the time which is near one shall come unto thee and he shall be unto thee thy hand maiden - He shall serve within the temple as one humble of heart and swift of foot -

I say he shall serve in humbleness of heart and with joy - So great shall be his joy that his feet shall be swift and his hands shall serve in gratitude for his being -

Blest are they which serve with a glad heart - I am of a mind to bring him in and I shall be unto him great light - for he has served well within the place wherein I am - And I say he is not one to betray himself or his trust - I say he shall serve in gratitude for his being - He shall not betray himself or his trust -

Forget not that I have said he shall be as none other - He has not been with thee in this place nor has he been in any other temple which has come into the outer manifestation - He has gone out for the first time in many moons - I say he has been within the place wherein I am for the purpose which he shall now serve - I say for this part is he prepared - For this have I prepared him -

Now ye shall know him for I shall give unto thee a sign and ye shall not be deceived So shall ye receive him into thy place of abode as a brother and ye shall be glad for his coming - So be it and Selah -

I am going to place within thy hand a packet wherein there shall be a sign and that sign shall be his and when he comes ye shall recognize it and ye shall be unto him a sister and he unto thee a brother - And ye shall have no cause for tears - Blest are they which are sent unto thee in my name - I am sent of the Father and I come unto thee in His name and for 'their' sake do I come that they may become even as He, the Father - For He has given unto them free will and when they choose to return unto their rightful estate willed unto them of God the Father - He shall send one out to show the way - to bring them out of bondage - out of darkness wherein they have been bound -

I say the day is now come when they which are so prepared shall be as ones which have upon their head the Corona of the Sun and upon their forehead the Seal of Solomon - I say these shall step forth as the

Sons of God revealed - They shall not die, neither shall they taste of death - for death shall have no power over him - Blest is he which is lifted up in the name of the Father Son and Holy Ghost - Amen and Selah -

I am with thee unto the end - I am Sanat Kumara

> **Sister Thedra of the Emerald Cross**

Ye Shall Give His Shelter

Sanat Kumara speaking-

I say unto thee- My Own- As I have not said before- I now stand ready to bring unto thee one which stands with thee- which shall be unto thee thy shield and thy buckler and I say unto thee ye shall be as one which has my hand upon thee And I say ye shall be as one which has given of thyself that they may be blest-

Now ye shall give shelter unto He which is to come and He which shall be unto thee a hand and a foot- And I shall be unto him all that is necessary for he shall come unto thee as a Brother and he shall be as one which has a mind to serve the Christ- And he shall be as one sent of God the Father- And he shall stand by thee as one which has the will to serve the Light -

I say he shall serve the Light with all his strength and I say ye shall have cause for rejoicing- So let it be-

Amen and Selah -

I Am now prepared to bring him unto thee- So be it that he is now prepared- And I Am glad- So be it ye shall receive him in the name of the Father, Son and Holy Ghost- Amen and Selah

I Am Sanat Kumara

Sister Thedra of the Emerald Cross

Sanat Kumara speaking -

Beloved of my being - Blest art thou and blest shall ye be - And now ye shall be as one which has my hand upon thee and ye shall be blest even as I am blest -

Be ye as one prepared to receive him which shall come unto thee and ye shall be blest of him and by him -

I am within this place wherein I am as one prepared to send him - and for this is he prepared - And from this day forth shall ye be as one on whose shoulders rests the responsibility of this altar which has been set up within the outer place and in the name of the Most High Living God - So be it thy responsibility shall be great indeed - And I am with thee unto the end -

Now ye shall be as one which has the part of "---" and he shall have that of the "---" - And again I say that thy younger sister shall have the part of altar service - She shall attend the altar and prepare the service It shall be as that of no other for it shall contain a basin of fresh clean water - And it shall be as one which has cleansed the hands - And there shall be a glass and that glass shall contain fresh clean water - And each shall sip from it in remembrance of me - And I say I am of the Father sent that ye may drink of the goblet of life and I say ye each shall drink from the goblet - First thyself - Second unto thy right - And it shall pass from hand to hand until it is returned unto Wanica - which shall partake of the last drop and return it unto the altar -

I say the altar shall have upon it the linen which is new - virgin linen and used for nothing else - I say it shall be for the altar only -

Now ye shall come unto this altar in silence - And too I say ye shall be as one in authority - And when one among thee finds fault with this procedure he shall be excluded - I say I am of the mind to cast them out and they shall not come unto this altar with criticism upon their lips - or for the purpose of giving unto themself credit for being wise -

I say that I am the Master within this temple and I know that which I say and do - And I am not of a mind to give unto the foolish my pearls without price - I command of thee obedience in all things - I give unto thee a commandment this day - Be ye as one prepared to receive him which shall come unto thee and he shall come as one sent of God the Father -

I say he shall come unto thee for the purpose of serving the plan - He shall serve with all his strength - So be it and Selah -

I am with thee and I shall not forsake thee -

I am thy brother and thy Sibor - Sanat Kumara -

Sister Thedra of the Emerald Cross

Sanat Kumara speaking unto thee which is my hand made manifest unto them -

I say that they shall hear me - And they shall comprehend that which I say unto thee - For it is now come when ye shall be brought out from the places wherein ye are and ye shall find therein no hiding place And ye shall be as ones with no place to lay thy head - For within the time which is near ye shall be as the foxes and ye shall be as ones which have thrown overboard thy own life belt - for I say unto thee: ye have been told many times that the day of sorrow is neigh upon thee and yet ye are deep in lethargy -

And ye have not stirred within thy tracks - Ye have been as ones with feet of lead - Ye have moved as with leaden feet - Ye have been slothful in thy ways and ye have been as ones which have upon thy back the burden of the ass - And ye have been as the tillers of the soil which know not the seasons -

Ye have sown in the fallow places naught - Ye have sown in the fertile places naught - Ye have sown upon the rocks - Ye have given unto the winds the power to scatter thy grain and ye have squandered thy fortune - And ye have been found wanting - I say ye have squandered thy substance and I say ye have given of thy substance unto the thieves who would rob thee and who would call thee fools -

I say ye have given unto the thieves that which has made of thee paupers and ye have been as the foolish virgins - I say ye are now out of oil - I say ye have squandered thy substance - Such is a fool indeed.

I am not so foolish for I am now prepared to bring them out from among thee which are prepared for this part which shall be revealed unto the just and the prudent - And I say unto them - Be ye alert and ye shall bear witness of me and ye shall have upon thy head the Crown of the Sun and the Seal of Solomon shall be upon thy forehead - So be it and Selah -

I am not so foolish as to waste my substance - for I am of the Father sent that ye may be brought out of bondage and that ye may have light abundantly - I say that ye shall have light abundantly which are so minded to follow me - For I shall lead thee into the place wherein I shall reveal many things unto thee - which are prepared for such revelation -

I am he which is responsible for this new dispensation - for I have brought it forth from out the inner temple wherein the Father is - So be it I am he which is known as the Most Worthy Grand Master -

So be it - Amen and Selah -

I am thy Sibor and thy older brother - Sanat Kumara -

Sister Thedra of the Emerald Cross

Sanat Kumara speaking:

Be ye blest of my presence - For I am come that ye may be blest - And I say unto thee this house shall be blest this night - for one has come into it who shall be as one on whose brow shall rest the symbol of Peace - I say on his brow shall rest the symbol of Peace - And that peace shall be unto him his shield and his buckler -

I say he shall be blest for the presence which is and which he shall come to recognize - I say by my presence shall he be blest -

So be it he shall come to know me and he shall come to know that which shall be unto him his passport into the secret places of my abode for I say he shall pass within these portals as one which knows and he shall know that he knows - And such is wisdom - So be it and Selah -

I am now prepared to give unto him a part which shall be unto him great wisdom - Great shall be his light - So be it and Selah -

Now say unto him as I would say that he shall bring forth one from out the south wherein he shall go - which shall be unto me my hand made manifest unto them and he shall be as one which has gone into the southland as for to bring back this one -

I say that the one which has the fortune to be unto him his <u>mate</u> shall be unto them my hand made manifest unto the ones which have a mind to learn - And he shall be as one which shall be unto her - her hand maiden -

She shall do that which shall be commanded of her - And he shall be unto her that which shall be commended of him - And they shall work as a team – Such is wisdom -

I say unto him he has found his way into this place as part of the plan - So be it and Selah -

I am thy older brother - Sanat Kumara

Sister Thedra of the Emerald Cross

Sanat Kumara speaking:

Beloved of my being - I am come that ye may be blest this day - And I say unto thee ye shall be blest - For one shall come unto thee which has my hand upon him and he shall be unto thee thy hand and thy feet - And he shall be as none other has been - He shall be as one on whose shoulders shall rest the responsibility of thy welfare -

I say he shall take upon him the responsibility of thy welfare and he shall be unto thee that for which he is sent - I say he is sent of God the Father that this plan may be brot forth - Such is the plan for him and he shall not fail thee - Nor shall he betray himself or his trust -

I am now prepared to bring him unto thee and ye shall be glad - So be it and Selah - I am with thee unto the end -

Now ye shall say unto the one which has within his hand that which shall be given unto him that he shall go in peace and I shall direct him and he shall follow the directions which I shall give unto him -

He shall go straightway and not tarry for naught - He shall return immediately and when he arrives at his destination in the north I shall speak unto the one which shall be my hand made manifest and I shall put into her mouth the words which shall be unto him the words of wisdom -

I say thru her I shall direct him - Yet he shall not forget from whence his blessings - I say he shall remember the ones which haven prepared the way before him - I say I shall direct him - yet he shall be mindful at all times of his blessings - He shall give unto the Father credit for his being and unto his benefactors credit for his well-being -

I am within the place wherein I am prepared to reveal many things unto him - And I say he shall be as one alert and mindful of all his blessings and the Source thereof - So shall it profit him -

I am thy Sibor and I have spoken - So be it - And be it so -

I am Sanat Kumara

Sister Thedra of the Emerald Cross

TO THE ONES IN HIGH PLACES

Sanat Kumara speaking -

Ye shall now give unto them this word and it shall go out unto all which are of a mind to learn -

I say unto them that it is now come when they shall be as ones which have burned the midnite oil and they have wasted their substance for they have sown unto the wind - They have been as the ones which have gathered unto themself tares and thistles - I say they have wasted their substance - And they have not taken thought of the Father which has given unto them being - Now I say unto them they have given unto themself credit for being wise when they have been the greatest of fools I say they have been fools -

Now I say unto them which sit in high places that there are none so foolish as the one which thinks himself wise and none so sad as he which betrays himself or his trust - for it is now come when the traitors shall be brought to account for his foolishness - and he shall be as one cast out - I say he shall be as one cast out - For he has not reckoned with the law - He has not given credit where credit is due - He has not been unto himself true -

Nor has he been unto his trust true - He has been unto himself traitor He has bartered in human sacrifice - He has been as one which has upon his hand the blood of the saints - the blood of his children and the blood of his brother - I say he has even sacrificed his father and mother that he be given the privilege of serving the one cast down - the dragon - I say he shall come to know that which has held him bound hand and foot to be the dragon - which has gone the long way to bind him -

Now I say unto thee which have a mind to learn that there are none so sad as the one which betrays his trust - for he shall suffer the consequences - And he shall be as one cast out -

For the first time I say unto them which betray themself that they shall go unto a place which is prepared for them wherein they shall begin at the beginning - They shall have their memory blanked from them and they shall know not that which they now boast of - the knowledge of which they boast shall be as naught - And all their opinions shall go as the chaff before the wind -

I speak unto them which are so minded to serve the forces of darkness - and when ye have given of thyself that ye may be glorified and thy appetites satisfied ye shall be as ones which have given of thy strength and of thy self that thy brother may suffer that which is unbearable - And I say woe unto any man which gives unto his brother the bitter cup - Such is my word unto thee and ye shall study well these my words - for ye shall have cause to remember them -

I am come that they may be delivered up which have a mind unto peace and them which have a mind unto learning I shall give unto them wisdom and peace which no man shall take from them and I am of the mind to give unto them as I have received of the Father - Such is my inheritance that I am one with the Father and all the Father has is mine to give - for He has endowed unto me all that He is and all that He has And for this do I say - Be ye as one prepared for to receive me and of me - for inasmuch as ye do receive me ye shall receive the Father and as ye receive Him and of Him - So shall ye receive thy Godhood - Amen and Selah. - I am thy older brother - Sanat Kumara

Sanat Kumara speaking - Unto thee which are at this altar -

I say unto thee ye shall be as ones which have within thy hands the keys unto the place wherein I am - And I say unto thee ye shall carry them gently and with dignity - I shall command of thee gentleness and such as is becoming of my fortunes - I say ye have been fortuned unto me - And ye have been given unto me for a purpose - And I say ye have the power to tie my hands - And when ye are as wayward children I am bound to step aside as one which shall wait for thee to grow up - to become of the age of accountability - For I have said I give not my pearls of price unto babes who know not their worth -

Now ye shall remember these my words and mark them well - for I am not of a mind to sibor fools - I keep my word - And I am not so minded to come into the places wherein there are ones which have upon their heads the scorpion - And upon their heart the scars which they have engraved by their own unknowing - which they CARRY AS THE ROSARIES - I say they which do carry the scars of bygone day as something to be cherished as the ROSARY shall be as the wonton - And such are not yet ready to receive me -

I say ye shall this day forgive thyself all thy childishness and all thy pettishness and turn from them as ye would from the termite - it undermines the very foundation on which ye are to build this temple -

I say that this temple shall stand - And when it is come that one is found unfit to be the foundation upon which it is builded that block shall be removed - And I say it is the fortune of me to know wherein is another - So be it and Selah -

I am Sanat Kumara -

Sister Thedra of the Emerald Cross

Sanat Kumara speaking unto thee beloved Sister of the Emerald Cross Be ye as one which has my hand upon thee and ye shall be blest of me and by me - For I say unto thee ye shall be as one prepared for the part which shall now be given unto thee - And for this part have ye been prepared -

Ye shall now go into all the lands of the earth and give unto them as ye have received and ye shall be unto them my hand and my mouth for I shall give unto thee the gift of speech and ye shall be blest of me and by me - And ye shall say unto them that which I shall give unto thee to say - And I say unto thee great shall be thy responsibility - for I say great shall be the responsibility of them which have within their hand the keys unto the kingdom - And I say the keys shall be put into thy hand - And so great shall be the responsibility that ye shall tremble within thy tracks -

I say unto thee fear not for I shall be with thee unto the end and ye shall have my hand upon thee and I shall sustain thee - Blest shall ye be and blest shall they be which are with thee and I say I shall give unto them that they may be sustained in their search - And I say they shall search within themself - For within them lie the secret unto their freedom -

Be ye forever alert and mindful of thy Source and be ye not as one which has thy hand upon the cup and drop it into the pit - I say drop it not - Carry it with care - And treasure it, for too I say be ye mindful of thy treasure - Let it not slip from the tips of thy fingers - And bear this in mind that all thy being has its beginning and its end within the Father-Mother God - And ye are but the ray sent out which shall return unto Him - Bother not with trifles and be ye of a mind to learn - And great shall be thy reward -

I am thy servant and thy brother - Sanat Kumara -

Senanda speaking:

Now it is come when ye shall be as ones which have gone the long way to bless them - And for this do I speak with thee at this time - When ye have given of thy effort and of thy strength ye have been as ones which have chosen this part - And when ye have given of thy heart ye have done well -

And ye shall now be as ones which have my hand upon thee for I shall bless thee and I shall give unto thee of my own account that ye may be blest - For I am now come that ye may have the part which has been kept for thee and ye shall be as ones which shall have thy hand in mine and ye shall be led into a place which is new unto thee - And strange shall it be - And by my hand shall ye be led - I say ye shall be led into a place wherein ye have not been - for it is now come when ye shall be brought into a new place wherein ye have not been - And I say not one which ye have known has been in the place of which I speak - I say ye have not been within it nor has any of the others -

Now ye shall walk into this place as ones in flesh and bone and as ones prepared for a new part - I say ye shall have a new part and ye shall be glad - So be it and Selah - Now ye shall be as one which have the will to learn and ye shall have many things revealed unto thee - So be it and Selah - I am thy Sibor and thy brother - Sananda

Sister Thedra of the Emerald Cross

Sanat Kumara speaking -

Blessed one - Be ye blest of my presence and I say unto thee ye shall be blest for it is now come when ye shall be brought out from the place wherein ye are into the place wherein I am and ye shall receive of me as I have received of the Father - So be it and Selah -

Now I have said I am prepared to bring thee in and to give unto thee as ye are prepared to receive - And I say ye have been prepared for thy new part - Such is thy part that ye shall give unto them as ye have received - So be it that they too shall be blest -

I say unto them they too shall receive as they are prepared - And I say each and every one which has a mind to learn shall be given as he is capable of receiving - Yet I say none shall pilfer my secrets -

I say too there are no secrets other than thy un-knowing - for when ye truly know ye shall know and know that ye know - And I say that none think which are wise - They know - and know that they know - Now be ye as ones which have my hand upon thee and I shall bless thee and I shall give unto thee as ye are capable of receiving - Such is wisdom -

I have set before thee the law and ye shall study well that which is given unto thee - Such is wisdom -

Blest are they which cometh into this house and blest shall ye be for having them - I have said unto thee that none shall be turned away. So be it and Selah -

I am Sanat Kumara -

Sister Thedra of the Emerald Cross

Sananda speaking -

Beloved of my being - Be ye blest of my being for I come unto thee of the Father which has given unto me being that ye may be blest even as I have been blest -

Now let this be recorded even as I say it unto thee for it shall be for the good of all mankind that which I say unto thee -

Have I not been mindful of thee and have I not given unto thee a part which has been kept for this day - Was it not said that ye have been spared for this day that ye might fulfill thy mission in this day?

Now ye shall be as one blest - for within the time which is near ye shall walk with me and talk with me - And ye shall go and come even as I go and come - I say ye shall go and come even as I go and come - And ye shall be as I am for ye shall be free even as I am free - I say ye shall be free even as I am free - for there shall be many which shall come unto thee that ye may be free - I say many shall come unto thee for the purpose of preparing thee for the greater part - Is it not said this is the path of initiation - And is it not?

Now let it be recorded that there are none so foolish as the one which thinks himself wise and none so sad as the one which betrays himself or his trust -

And for this have I said - Be ye true unto thyself and seek ye first the Kingdom of God and all these things shall be added unto them - And I say that all these things are as naught in the Father's place of abode - for these things shall pass away as no-thing - And I say that when ye have passed through these portals ye shall be given the power and the authority to create like unto the Father - And ye shall have the wisdom and the power which is His -

And ye shall reach out thy hand and command that which ye will and the elements shall be unto thee thy faithful and obedient servant - They shall obey in love and harmony and ye shall create good - And ye shall be blest of God the Father for He has so willed that ye glorify Him in the earth - And I say for this has many been sent unto thee that this may be accomplished - Amen - So be it and Selah -

Give unto the Father all the credit and all the praise now and ever more - So be it and Selah -

I am thy brother and thy Sibor - Sananda Son of God - Amen - So be it -

Sister Thedra of the Emerald Cross

Sanat Kumara speaking -

This day I would give unto thee one commandment - Be ye as ones which have within the rod which shall become brass -

I say within thy hand is the key unto the place wherein the Father abides -

Be ye as ones which can comprehend that which I have said unto thee -

I say ye shall be as ones which have the mind to walk in the way set before thee -

Ye shall turn from thy childishness - And ye shall grow into maturity -

Ye shall put away thy small ways and ye shall be as adults which have upon thy heads the Crown of the Sun and ye shall walk which way it tilts not -

I say ye shall now walk as ones which have within thy hands a lamp which has been lit within a dark place and I say ye shall carry that lamp high and ye shall be custodian of it - Ye shall guard it well and watch that an ill wind does not extinguish it -

I say ye have been made custodian of the lamp which flickers dimly in a dark place and ye shall feed that flame from thy own oil - I say from thy own oil shall ye feed it - Ye shall give thy attention unto this which I say unto thee - Ye shall practice that which I give unto thee - Ye shall not turn from the way set before thee - I say woe unto any man which turneth back -

I have given unto thee commandments which ye have not lived to the fullest - And ye shall this day begin thy search for the key which lies within these commandments - and ye shall be as one which has betrayed himself when ye pass them by lightly -

I say ye shall turn back each and every page and find them one by one and practice them until they become thy very nature - I say this is thy key into the secret place of the most high living God -

For none enter into His place of abode unprepared - So be it that He has accepted thee - Yet ye shall not enter unprepared -

Too I say this is the day of preparation and I say all within the place wherein I am have come that ye may be brought in - Yet ye and ye alone shall prepare thyself - And when ye are so prepared one shall come unto thee and give unto thee as ye are prepared to receive -

I say we are not so foolish as to give of our pearls unto babes who know not their worth -

I say when ye grow to maturity and when ye become accountable for all thy actions one shall come unto thee and give unto thee as ye are prepared to receive - No more - No less - I am thy older brother - Sanat Kumara -

Sister Thedra of the Emerald Cross

Sanat Kumara speaking unto thee beloved ones which have remembered this hour - Have ye not remembered it for thy own sake? Have ye not been unto thyself true for this moment? I see thee as ones laboring late and with weary hands for the sake of others that they may know that which is given unto thee -

Ye shall now say unto them in my name that they which are of a mind to learn shall be as ones prepared for the great learning - for it is now come when I shall speak thru the ones which have prepared themself for this part - I shall be as one which has the power and the authority to give unto them such gifts as speech - hearing and writing - I shall be withhold that of sight for the time - for it is the better part of wisdom -

Now say unto them that when it is come that they are given such gifts as hearing and speaking and writing they shall be as ones which have great responsibility - For I say great shall be the responsibility of anyone which so ever that takes up the banner of Truth - For I say the truth shall be as the pearl without price - I say that they dive deep for the pearl without price -

I say that they pay for every pearl - Yet I say ye cannot buy with thy puny coin this pearl of which I speak - for it is truly without price -

Therefore I guard it well - I treasure my heritage - I am not a fool! I waste not my substance nor my inheritance which the Father has willed unto me - I say they which do are fools indeed -

Now I say that they which do receive such gifts shall abide by the law of Love, Truth and Justice - They shall walk in the Light of the Christ and turn not to the left nor to the right - They shall be responsible for their actions and for that which they send out - They shall be as ones on whose shoulders rest the responsibility of all their words and in all their deeds - And I say woe unto anyone which so ever who puts words into my mouth -

I have seen this done and I say I spew them out - I say I am not about to be given the bitter cup - I am not easily prompted to offense - Yet I say they do offend me - And my love alone keeps me from saying that which ye would say - Yet I am mindful of their weakness and of their unknowing - Yet I say that when they are confronted with their foolishness they shall be as ones plagued by it - They shall be as ones brought up short - I say they shall come to know that which they have done and they shall be held accountable for their foolishness - So be it and Selah -

Now I say unto thee my hand made manifest - Ye shall send this out and I say the seed planted in fertile soil shall grow as the banyan tree and great shall be the harvest thereof - I say ye shall be blest of me and by me and ye shall sign all these documents thusly -

Sister Thedra of the Emerald Cross

Sanat Kumara speaking -

Blest art thou and blest shall ye be - For I am come that ye may be blest - Now ye shall see that which shall be given unto thee to see - And ye shall recognize it for what it is - I say ye shall now see that which shall be shown thee through revelation - I say many things shall be revealed unto unto thee and ye shall know and know that ye know -

Be ye as one prepared for such revelation - I say ye shall have many things revealed unto thee and ye shall be as ones which have prepared thyself for such revelation - It is said that revelation is a gift of God the Father - Given unto thee as part of thy inheritance - So it is - And so be it a great gift indeed - Yet I say unto thee wisdom is the greatest of all So be it when ye have become wise ye shall be able to control the elements and ye shall go out from the earth as one unbound and ye shall have free concourse into all the planets of the galaxy and ye shall move freely without any apparatus other than that which ye create from the eth - Ye shall be as one in full command -

Ye shall create from the virgin eth - And ye shall need no machinery, no gadgets - Ye shall be master of the elements - Ye shall command them and they shall obey thee in Love - Peace - and Harmony.

This has been given unto the Sons of God as part of their inheritance I say when ye are brot before the great white altar wherein I am ye shall be as one which has prepared thyself for this part - Ye shall stand before this altar and I shall declare for thee thy freedom and ye shall be as one freed from all bondage - Forever free!

Blest are they which do receive their freedom for they shall see God So be it the will of God the Father -

Now ye shall send this out that they may bear witness of these my words - For it is as my words made manifest unto thee and as they prepare themself so shall they receive -

It is said that when one stands upon the holy ground wherein stands the altar of white alabaster that they are never the same - So be it a truth Yet I say some do wait for yet another day - and some do become overly anxious and they do become sick at heart and fall - and become bruised and they are not to be censored for they are but the ones which would rush in where angels fear to tread - I say they who try to storm the gates of the temple are foolish indeed - for they find it not - Is it not said he that which comes any other way is a liar and a thief? I say he is not permitted to enter these portals without the proper credentials - And I am the gate keeper - And I watch with diligence that none pilfer the secrets which shall be revealed unto the just and the worthy -

I am not in lethargy nor am I a fool - I keep watch over my own - I do not sacrifice my own - I do know them and I guard them by day and by night - Yet I say be ye as ones prepared for the greater part for this is thy inheritance in full - So be it and Selah -

I am come that ye may be brought out this day - So be it I am glad it is come when I may come in and council with thee and speak with thee thusly - So be it I shall speak with thee when ye are prepared to receive me -

Yet I shall say woe unto anyone which so ever who puts words into my mouth for I shall spew them out and great shall be thy sorrow -

I am within the place wherein I am prepared for this day - And none shall take from me the word - Nor add unto -

I am thy Sibor and thy brother -

Sanat Kumara

Sister Thedra of the Emerald Cross

The following message was channeled through Sorea Sorea from Unit #3.

Dear ones: As ye have come together in answer to the call that was made to thee, ye shall be blessed.

It has been given to this one, Monea, to call thee together and those who respond to this call shall be given the greater part which has been kept for them. Ye shall pray much and prepare thyselves for it is the greater part of wisdom to be prepared. Ye shall be richly rewarded for thy work in that measure which is given, and ye who answer not the call and prepare not for the service required of thee shall be rewarded in like measure.

These calls are not lightly given nor do I ask in an idle mood. The work is great and the workers badly needed. Therefore, do not betray thyself by taking any call that is given thee as of no importance. I do not call without a purpose.

Make obedience thy watchword, heed and ponder the words that are given unto thee and ye shall have thy reward and ye shall rejoice.

So be it and Selah - I am thy brother - Sananda

Sanat Kumara speaking -

Blest art thou my child - And blest shall they be which read these my words - For this shall I give them unto thee that they may receive them through thee - Such is my hand made manifest unto them -

Now say unto them as I would say that with my being I bless them and with my presence I bless them -

I say because I am I do bless them and for this do I speak unto thee my Sister of the Emerald Cross - that they too may come to know me and that they too may be prepared to receive me - and of me - For it is now come when I shall manifest in physical for the purpose of giving unto the world that for which they have waited -

I say I have waited long for this day when I shall speak thusly - And it is now come when I shall come unto thee in flesh and bone and I shall council thee as one of thy own* - I say ye shall be as one prepared to receive me - for I say I am now prepared to come unto thee as one of thy own - For this have ye waited - Now ye shall receive me and of me And ye shall be glad for thy preparation - So be it and Selah - Now ye shall say unto them that when they are sufficiently prepared I shall come unto them and I shall council them and I shall give unto them a gift far more precious than frankincense and myrrh -

Now I say one shall come unto thee from out the place wherein I am and he shall be unto thee thy hand and thy foot - I say he shall be unto thee all that the Father would have him be - And he shall bless thee and he shall give unto thee that which is wise and prudent - So be it and Selah -

Blest are they which come in the name of the Father Son and Holy Ghost -

I say I shall send one out from the place wherein I am as one prepared to give unto thee that which the Father would have him give unto thee - And ye shall be glad to receive him and it shall profit thee much -

I am with thee that the Father's will might be done in us and thru us. So be it we shall glorify him within the earth - Hallelujah -

* As mortal man

* * * * * * * *

Sananda speaking -

Beloved of my being - I speak after my beloved brother Sanat Kumara - For the purpose which has been withheld for this time have I not spoken for a short time - Now I too shall open my mouth and I shall say unto thee that which is prompted by love, wisdom and mercy - I have come at this moment that ye may be blest - And too I say the others shall be blest - For have they too not come unto this altar that they might receive their part - I say they too shall be blest -

Too I say all which take within their heart these my words shall be blest of me and by me - I say they which open up their heart I shall touch them and they shall receive me unto themself - I say they shall receive me unto themself -

Now for this do I speak unto thee that they may come to know me by my new name - for I say it is now the new day - the new age - when the old shall pass away and all things shall be made new - I say all things shall be made new - And ye shall remember these my words for ye shall have cause to remember them -

When ye have remembered them ye shall look deep within thyself and search out that which lies within the secret place and ye shall rid thyself of all that which is unto thyself the gross of which ye have garnered unto thyself - which is thy legirons and unto thee thy own pitfalls - I say all the pitfalls are within thy own self -

I say cleanse thy place of abode - Cleanse thy place of abode and prepare thyself for the greater part -

Wherein is it said that there is none so sad as the one which betrays himself - I speak unto thee from the depth of my very being - I cry a loud unto the Father that He may give unto me of His grace that ye may be delivered out -

I say ye have slept overtime and I now give unto thee a key and ye have but to turn it within the gate - For I say ye shall pass from the pore into the Holy Christ body as one made new - As one made whole - As one purified - When ye have learned the law which governs thy being I say the key is but this: Love thy life which the Father has endowed unto thee - and thy freedom is assured thee -

Blest are they which learn this lesson - Fortune unto thyself such love - And I say ye shall stand free even as I am free -

I bless thee and I give unto the Father thanks that He has allowed me the privilege of coming unto thee - So be it I shall praise Him forever - Amen and Selah -

I am He which was born of Mary and the word of Joseph - Called Jesus the Christ known within this temple as Sananda - Son of God - So be it and Selah -

* * * * * * * * *

He which is without sound speaketh: and blessings upon thee my child I come unto thee from out the silence - I come unto thee from out the silence that all men may know that which I know -

I say that upon this day and within this thy year of 1962 I have come unto thee from out the silence wherein I have performed many ceremonies without words - I say my work is without words - for I am the Master of Vibration which is soundless - I move without sound - I am motion - I create by motion - Within motion I create - I move - I create - I create as I move -

I go out without sound - I am soundless - I am movement - I go in with no sound - I go out without sound - I go out from the great void wherein is no sound - I move upon the eth - I go into the depth wherein is no sound - I move and there becomes sound -

I am he which creates from the depth of silence - I bring forth - I go into the great void wherein is no thing and I move and there becomes -

I cause that which shall be - to become - I call forth from the depth of my being all which becomes - I call forth that which shall become worlds without end - I call forth that which I will and I give unto it vibration and NOTHING goes out from me without first having form -

I say nothing goes out from me without first having form -

I call forth form and from myself I give it vibration and then it becomes that which is heard and seen - I say it first takes form then it is heard and seen within thy own dimension - I say first it becomes form within my realm and then it is seen and heard - and felt within thy realm.

I speak unto thee from out the silence - I speak without sound - yet ye have heard me - and recorded these my words that they which have ears to hear may hear them - I say that they have heard NOthing with their physical ears - for it is as nothing - I say they are as ones deaf - for they hear NOT with their physical ears -

Be ye blest for this my word unto them through thee - I say I shall give unto thee a gift and by that gift shall ye be known -

I am the one which has opened this door that this part may be added unto the others and this shall go out with that of the others of Sanat Kumara and Sananda - And ye shall say I am he which is without sound And I AM and I AM -

Sister Thedra of the Emerald Cross

Sanat Kumara speaking -

Now my beloved in the day which is now come ye shall take up thy pen as one which has upon thy head a crown and ye shall be given a part which shall be for the good of all mankind - And ye shall record that which is said unto thee - And I command thee give it unto THEM as it is spoken - for not one word shall be misplaced or mis-spoken - I say it shall reach the ones for which they are intended - for it shall be given from the Hiarchi (Hierarchy) - And it shall not be necessary to change it*- I say it shall reach the ones which are willing to receive it and it is in no wise the better part of wisdom to change one word -

Was it not given unto the foolish to change the words of the Scriptures many times? Have they not lost their essence and have they not lost the word** - And have they not given unto themself credit for being wise -

Now when ye have finished with this part ye shall give unto them permission to go*** - And ye shall prepare thyself for the part which shall be given unto thee as a part separate - And yet it shall go out unto them with this for this shall prepare "Them" which are prepared to receive this new part which shall be brot forth this day -

Now ye shall give unto "Them" the new part as it is spoken and ye shall be as one which has my hand upon thee - And I say woe unto any man which points a finger at thee - I now speak unto thee my recorder known unto us here within this temple as Sister Thedra of the Emerald Cross - Blest shall ye be for I shall bless thee with my presence and with my very being shall I bless thee by day and by night - So be it and Selah -

Blest are they which have come into this place wherein ye are and blest shall they be -

I am thy older brother and thy Sibor - Sanat Kumara

* This document

** The people have lost the Word

*** From this altar

* * * * * * * * * * * * * *

Eternal Mother am I - I am one which has given of my being that ye may have thy being - I am not separated from thee and I am not afar -

for I am thee - And thou art me - Blest art thou for I am blest and I am that which blesses and I am that which is blest - I bless myself and I give of myself that ye be blest - As my hands bless my feet I bless thee my child - I bless thee from the center of my being which ye are that which have gone out from me as the vine from it's root - I send unto thee the vine - life, and I sustain thee from the root which I am - I AM and I know that I AM and I am glad -

I say arise O my child and come unto me, thy eternal Mother and I shall give unto thee that which I have kept for thee - I say ye have waited long for thy inheritance which ye forfeited long ago -

Be ye as one which has my love, and my heart shall encompass thee in thy journey home - I say it is now come when ye shall be brought home as one free-forever free - And therein is cause for great joy - So be it the music shall ring out through all the cosmos - And THEY shall hear it and they shall see that which is given unto them to see - Yet they shall be in no wise wise - for they shall be as the sleepers - for they shall believe that which they see to be illusions of their own puny mind They shall think that they are dreaming -

And is it not so?

Now I say the sleepers shall sleep on while the ones which are awakened shall ascend unto me even as the Sons of God have returned unto me - I say the day of the new dispensation is come when they shall see that which is done openly and they shall not know that which they see - For they shall be as ones walking in their sleep - I say they which are awake shall be brought out of bondage this day - I say it is now come when one shall be sent from out the temple wherein stands the altar of white alabaster - which shall bring thee into the place wherein there shall stand a light which is LIVING LIGHT - It is life itself - It is undistinguishable and it is not a power of earth - It is the life force and that flame is the force from which cometh all fire - all warmth - And love is the feeling quality and that which motivates the Love Principle.

I am the Love Principle in action - I AM and I know myself to be Love in Action - I am love and I am ACTION - And because I AM thou art - And LOVE motivates thy every action and for this do I now make myself known unto thee - for this is my part with thee - to prepare thee for thy new part - And I have spoken unto thee many times and for this do ye now receive me and give unto me credit for that which I am -

Have ye not walked within the Temple of Fire - Have ye not walked upon the flame wherein ye were unharmed - I say ye have been blest - Yea even purified - Blest are they which have entered upon the steps of the Flame Temple wherein ye shall go - Blest am I to receive thee -

I shall say unto THEM that which ye will not - For it is given unto me to know the wisdom thereof - I am within the place wherein I abide as the Son or the Central Sun - from which ye have gone out - And I am within this place prepared to receive thee - Such is my joy and my great love shall enfold thee in thy preparation - I bless thee O my child.

Bring thyself unto this altar at a later hour and I shall speak with thee again this day -

And for this do I bring thee unto this altar - Bless thee my soul - Be ye as one come out from me - And be ye as one which has returned unto me -

Go NOT out from me and I shall make of thee a prophet in thy own right -

I shall bring thee back into me from whence ye have gone out - And therein I shall prepare a part for thee and ye shall with dignity and upon thy head shall be the Crown of the Sun and upon thy forehead the Seal of Solomon - And ye shall know as I know - For ye shall be one with me and I say ye shall return unto me in honor and with dignity - For such is the nature of my Sons which return unto me - And ye shall walk with me and ye shall talk with me and ye shall know thyself to be as I And I shall give unto thee all that I am - For I am thee and thou art me Such is my part to bring thee back from whence ye went out - And I say ye shall go out no more - So be it I am glad -

I am thy eternal Mother - So be it and Selah -

I known as Sara

Mother of Abraham

Sister Thedra of the Emerald Cross

Sanat Kumara speaking -

Blest art thou and blest shall ye be -

I say ye have come together for the purpose of bringing about order from out the chaos - And ye have been as ones working blindly for ye have walked step at a time - knowing not that which is ahead of thee - I say ye shall be as ones blest of me and by me - Yet ye shall walk in the way set before thee - Ye shall have upon thy shoulders the full responsibility of thy own progress - Ye shall apply thyself whole heartedly and ye shall not let any word of slander pass from thy lips -

Ye shall blame not one which is among thee for their unknowing - Ye shall be as one responsible for every word which passes from thy lips - Ye shall be held accountable for all thy words - And I say they shall return unto thee multiplied a thousand fold - For this do I speak unto thee thusly -

For I say ye shall be as one cursed of thy own words or ye shall be as one blest by them - I say ye shall count to 10 before ye say one word of which ye are not sure - Ask of thyself "Is this prompted by LOVE, PEACE AND HARMONY" -

I say it is the better part of wisdom to see the Light of the Christ and to turn from thy petty way - thy little way - And I shall council thee in greater things - So be it and Selah -

Bless thee O my soul - I am come that ye may be blest - Amen - So be it and Selah -

I am Sanat Kumara

Sister Thedra of the Emerald Cross

Sanat Kumara speaking -

Blest art thou and blest shall ye be - And for this do I come that ye may be blest -

I am <u>one</u> which has guided and guarded thee and I have watched thee struggle within the mire of the earth while she has gone through her many initiations - For has she not also gone through many - And have ye not likewise been with her?

Now I say ye shall stand with her through this her (the earth) time of initiation for she is going through a great and trying time of crisis so to speak - I say now - this moment - She is being held within our hand as a baby which is being lifted from the womb by Caesarian birth - I say she, the earth is being re-born and we thy guardians are responsible for her safety -

And I say each of us has been given certain responsibilities - certain parts - And for this have we been prepared - Now I say ye shall stand with us - As ones which has upon thy shoulders certain responsibilities And ye shall forget them <u>NOT</u> - For this is the day of action - "Preparation!!" - Days for the great revelation is now at hand - I say that the foolish shall say I am being prepared - For I say ye are preparing thyself - None other prepares thee - I say when ye have given thy whole heart - thy whole self - to thy preparation one shall come unto thee and give unto thee that for which ye have prepared thyself for to receive -

Now I say ye shall be as ones alert - For too I say ye shall be as one on whose shoulders rest the responsibility of thy brothers and thy sisters. Yet ye are not to be held accountable for their shortcomings - or for their part - Ye shall be mindful of thy own attitude of thy <u>tongue</u> - of thy appearances - Yes shall walk as the living example of an initiate - And ye are to remember at <u>ALL</u> <u>TIMES</u> why ye have come unto this place -------

I say woe unto anyone WHO-SO-EVER - which speaks lightly of this endeavor -- For the law is sure and swift - And I say it is a law -

that anyone - WHO-SOEVER he be which says as much as shall besmirch the sisters or the brothers shall pay for such foolishness -

Blest are they which walk in the way set before them -

Now I say unto thee ye have come together again for the purpose of learning the laws which have hitherto been hidden from thee - And I now say unto thee - When ye have learned this lesson well I shall reveal the next one unto thee -

Be ye alert and wise and I shall be unto thee Sibor and I shall council thee in the way of the wise - And I shall bless thee as I have been blest - Amen and Selah -

I am thy older brother - Sanat Kumara

Sister Thedra of the Emerald Cross

Sanat Kumara speaking -

Beloved ones which have come unto this altar which the Father has set up - I say unto thee - I am now prepared to give unto thee as ye are prepared to receive - I say when ye are so prepared I shall come unto thee and I shall council thee in wisdom and in love -

I say ye shall prepare thyself - for as ye prepare thyself - so shall ye receive - I say ye shall be unto thyself true and follow in the way set before thee -

Now it is come when there shall be great stress upon the earth and within the earth - For I say unto thee my beloved ones which are now within this temple - that as sure as ye are here before me, ye shall stand and bear witness of my words - that the forces which have been built up within the earth and about the earth shall break forth as with a mighty blast - I say that within the twinkling of an eye that the force which has built up in and about the earth shall give forth with one mighty blast - And it shall be for the reason that the traitors have willed it so -

I say that when they have gone the long way to serve the dragon they have betrayed themself - And too I say ye which now sit within this place which I have caused to be brought into manifestation - has the PEACE and the COMPREHENSION of me and that which I say unto thee - Ye shall give more attention unto thy part - And ye shall be as ones alert unto thy part which has been given unto thee because ye have asked for this part - I say of thy own choice have ye been given this part - I say ye have volunteered for this part - and ye have forgotten thy choosing - Such is the pity of thy memory being blanked from thee I say the pity of it is the blanking of thy memory - And too I say ye which will it so shall have it restored -

Now if ye so will it ye shall be as ones given a new part. And for this have ye been brought into this place - And in the time which is near one shall come into this place which has the power and the authority to give unto thee - great and wise <u>instructions</u> - And ye shall be wise indeed to follow them -

I say ye shall not be opinioned nor shall ye be deceived - For I have given unto my hand made manifest the word which shall be unto her the key - I say she shall know him and ye shall be as one wise indeed to hear that which she says unto thee - For I have sibored her wisely - Such is my word unto thee -

I say go from this altar filled with joy and love - I say I shall bless thee with my being -

I am thy older brother - Sanat Kumara -

Sister Thedra of the Emerald Cross

Sanat Kumara speaking - Sananda speaks unto thee from out the silence Be ye blest by her presence for she speaks out the fullness of her heart for that purpose - I say ye shall be blest by her and of her being - Ye shall record for them that which she shall say unto thee and they shall bear witness of her words unto thee -

Be ye as one filled with compassion for him which has gone from this altar - for he is now given unto much sorrow and torment - I say he has gone from this altar of his own free will and by his own choice has he gone - Yet he has upon his own shoulders the responsibility of his own free will - For the first time it is said unto thee - He shall return - So be it and Selah -

I am with thee unto the end - So be it and Selah - Ye shall go and do that which shall be done -

Now ye shall give unto them these words of the beloved Sananda and she shall say unto them that which shall bless them -

* * * *

Beloved of my being - I come from out the silence that ye may be blest Be ye aware of me and these my words for they shall be a link between us - Ye shall come to know me as I know thee - I say ye shall come to know me and I shall council thee- for it is given unto me to be the compliment of our beloved Sanat Kumara - I am known by many names Yet I say ye shall know me by this name -

I have given unto thee this name for a purpose which shall serve thee well - Ye shall remember me in the days to come for I shall come unto thee in the days of stress and for this am I prepared -

Now for the first time I speak unto thee thru this temple and at this altar - And I say unto thee in wisdom and with great love - that ye have been brought together for the purpose which ye as yet do not know -

Ye are as yet following in darkness - Ye walk - one step at a time - And I say unto thee my beloved ones - Ye do not walk alone - for many times my hand is upon thee in loving silence - I see thy tears of joy - and of disappointment - I see thy struggles - I know thy poltices and I know where thy strength lies - I say ye shall come to know as I know and ye shall be glad for thy knowing -

Wherein is it said that there shall be one sent from out the temple wherein stands the great white altar - to help thee in thy struggle - and to give unto thee the plan which as yet has not been fully revealed unto thee - I say blest are they which do endure -

I am come that my light may bless and sustain thee - I say unto thee ye shall have within thee the fortitude to endure - And be ye mindful of thy benefactors and of thy own divinity - Walk as the Son of God the Father and I shall give unto thee a part and ye shall be glad - I am thy older sister and thy Sibor - Sananda

Sister Thedra of the Emerald Cross

Tarman of Allecea speaking -

Blest art thou - Blest shall ye be and be it so and so be it - I am with thee and I shall be with thee unto the end -

Be ye as one which has my hand upon thee - O my soul be thou blest by the Father-Mother God - I AM - and I AM forever and eternally one with thee - Oh my soul praise Him forever and forever more - I come unto thee that ye may be blest as I have been blest - I say unto thee ye shall receive of God the Father as I have received and give unto Him all the praise and the glory forever - and forever - Allejulia - Praise His Holy Name ----

Blest art they which come unto the altar which has been set up in His name and blest shall they be -

And now it is come when ye shall sing the Songs of Solomon - for I shall bless thee with my being and I shall give unto thee the gift of Solomon - I shall adorn thy head with pearls and rubies and sapphires shall I give unto thee - I shall give unto thee the sardonyx for thy breast plate - I shall give unto thee a ring for thy hand and in it shall be a planet and it SHALL be called Fortune of the Sons of God - And on it shall be written these words:

And therein is the symphony of the spheres - Be ye blest Oh My Soul - for I have sung unto thee my song in holy adoration - And ye shall give it unto them that they may bear witness - One shall set it to music and it shall glorify the Father - So be it and Selah -

I am thy Sibor and thy older brother - Tarman of Allecea -

Sister Thedra of the Emerald Cross

Sananda speaking -

Beloved of my being - Ye come unto this altar this morning that ye may be given light and in abundance - I say ye shall have it - And ye shall glorify the Father in the earth and ye shall be unto Him his mouth For ye shall say the words which He shall put into thy mouth and ye shall be unto Him His hand made manifest unto THEM - For He shall give unto thee the power and the authority to write that which He has for them and ye shall <u>change</u> <u>no</u> <u>word</u> - for it is the greatest of folly -

I say <u>not</u> <u>one</u> <u>word</u> shall be changed - So be it there is a law governing such things - Ye have been commanded obedience in all things and ye have kept the commandments given thee - Ye have made haste to obey and I am glad - for it is the better part of wisdom - May the Father see fit to give unto <u>them</u> the same comprehension -

I say they which ask of Him shall have comprehension - Yet they shall learn to prepare themself for such as He has willed unto them -

I say great are their leg irons - which are the things they fortune unto themself - Such as their Karma - their opinions - their wonton - their very rebelliousness is sufficient to keep them short of their course.

Blest are they which turn from their own wonton way and they which do turn unto the Source of their being for Light shall be as ones blest forevermore - They shall see God face to face - So be it and Selah.

When they do turn from their own wonton way they shall have their leg irons cut away - They shall be blest forever more - They shall find Peace such as they have not known -

I come not to bring Peace - but to make way for Peace - I give not unto the wonton - I give unto the ones which prepare themself to receive me - I ask of them only their will to learn and their hand - that I might lead them out of bondage - I lead gently - Yet I demand of them "Pick up thy feet! And walk - Drag not thy feet."

For I am not the burro - Ye ride NOT my back! Ye are created in the image of God the Father and ye are commanded - "Let thy own Light Shine"

"Let thy own Light Shine"

"Let thy own Light Shine"

And I am one sent of God the Father that ye may find thy way home. I am <u>one</u> of the way showers -

And I have been called by many names - Yet in this new day - this new dispensation I return unto them which have heard my voice and invited me in - as Sananda -

Yet there are many which deny me by any name - I say it is now come when they which are prepared to receive me and of me shall come to know me as Sananda - Son of God - I come as such - I shall go as such and I would that all which are upon the earth today might go as I go - Yet I have said that I have come that my covenant might be fulfilled with the Father and with thee -

And that some shall go into their new places of abode knowing not that I have ever come into the earth as man - And they are the ones which shall not know that there is a place prepared - for them -

I say that there are yet others, which call themself CHRISTIAN which shall go into their new places denying that I am come - And that I AM the Son of God - And that I am not as yet come - They shall deny me and these my words - And I say unto thee - These are the ANTICHRISTS - spoken of in thy Scriptures -

I say they are the ANTI-CHRISTS - spoken of in thy Scriptures -

I say be ye alert - And be ye aware of them for they lay for thee many a snare -

Blest are they which hold fast for I shall be with them unto the end and I am thy Sibor and thy brother -

For thy sake have I spoken unto them and ye shall give unto them as ye have received -

I am Sananda - Once known as Jesus Christ - Born of Mary and the ward of Joseph -

Blest are they - Amen and Selah-

Sister Thedra of the Emerald Cross

Father Solen speaking:

Behold me - I AM - and I AM and shall ever be -

I AM GOD - I AM He which IS and which shall ever be -

Behold me - Because I AM, thou art - Behold me in all that ye are and I have given unto thee being - And because I AM thou art - Behold me - and give unto me credit for being that which I AM and give unto thyself credit for being MY SON -- MY SON -

For I have given of myself that ye may have being and because ye are in me and have thy being in me - Ye are of me and ye ARE me - Behold me and give unto thyself credit for being a Son of God thy Father -

I say rejoice this day that ye have received thy Sonship which I have willed unto thee -

Behold my handiwork and rejoice - Rejoice forever more for I say unto thee ye shall see me face to face - Hallelujah - Amen

Say I unto thee ye shall return unto me even as ye went out - perfect in all things and I say ye shall behold me face to face - I say for this shall ye rejoice forever more - Hallelujah -

Blest are they which return unto me this day - I say unto thee my child blest are they which return this day -

Blest are MY SONS -

Amen and Selah -

I am thy Father Solen

So be it and be it so -

Sister Thedra of the Emerald Cross

Sanat Kumara speaking -

Beloved of my being - I come unto thee this morning that they may receive of me as ye have received - I say ye have received of me and by me - yet they have not touched the sleeve of my garment - for they have been as ones asleep - They stir slightly and they are yet dreaming while others are dead upon their feet!

I say that the dead walk among thee - They are as ones motivated and animated by the Astral World - I say the sleepers are as ones walking about as ones animated of the Astral World - they know not! They "think" and they give unto themself credit for being wise when they are fools indeed - for they are not the ones they believe themself to be - !

They have wandered long in darkness and they have not the will to awaken - They have thought themself wise and they give unto themself great and impressive titles and degrees dictated of man - and because of these things they call themselves "Master" -

I ask of thee - Are they? Wherein can they heal the sick - Wherein can they add one cubit unto their height - Wherein can they stay the elements - Wherein can they give sight unto the blind - Or wherein can they give unto the dying comfort?

Answer them the questions which they ask of thee when they come And give unto them no proof for I say unto thee they shall come and they shall demand proof - Yet I say - Give unto them NONE! For it shall be given unto the ones which are prepared and unto none other and I say the one so prepared demands NO proof - and the one which is not prepared shall have it NOT!!

Blest are they which do receive proof - for he has prepared himself to receive it -

I am come that he might have it -

Blest art thou my hand made manifest - for ye shall see me face to face -

I AM and I AM - forever one with the Father which has caused me to be Amen - So be it and Selah -

I am Sanat Kumara

Sister Thedra of the Emerald Cross

Sananda speaking -

Beloved of my being - Go into all the lands of the earth and say unto them these words - Blest shall they be which receive them and blest shall ye be - Blest are my servants for I shall glorify them even as the Father has glorified himself in me - Such is my word unto thee -

Now say unto them as I would and in my name that - They shall awaken! For it is now time that they arise and come forth - I say they shall awaken!

And too I say they shall have great pains in the process for I say they have fortuned unto themself much UNREST while they have slept and they shall be as ones rudely awakened - And they shall wonder why they have slept so late - I say it is later than they know - for the time is NOW and NOW is the time -

I say this is the time which has been spoken of in the Scriptures - for it is the Battle of Armageddon - when the forces of dark have within their hand the power to destroy thy planet earth - And I say that they shall be staid - Even at the cost of much sorrow - I say sorrow there shall be - And too I say all which are so minded to walk in the way set before them shall be brot out of bondage and they shall be as ones which are prepared for their deliverance from the torment which shall come upon the earth and unto the ones which are traitors unto themselves.

I say woe is he which does betray himself - And woe shall he be which gives unto his brother the bitter cup -

Blest are they which give unto me credit for being that which I am.

And I come that they may have light - Such is my mission at this time -

I am with thee that they may come to know me even as ye know me. So be it and Selah -

I am thy Sibor and thy brother - Sananda

* * * * * * * * *

Sanat Kumara speaking -

Blest are they which come unto this altar for the purpose of learning of the Father Son and Holy Ghost - For I say unto thee my children - Ye shall be blest even as we are blest which are within the place wherein I am -

I say unto this place ye shall come and ye shall know as we know - For I say none shall go unnoticed - for it is the law - When one is prepared for such learning he is found and brought in - And for this are we prepared - I say we are prepared for this day when there shall be a great gathering in and there shall be great joy and much gladness - For ye shall come to know of which I speak for I have said blest are they which come into the place wherein I am and I am within this place for the purpose of bringing thee in - So be it and Selah -

Blest are they which come for they shall receive of me as I have received of the Father Son and Holy Ghost - Amen and Selah -

I am Sanat Kumara

Sister Thedra of the Emerald Cross

Sanat Kumara speaking -

Beloved of my being - In this day shall ye be brought out of bondage - And ye shall be as one prepared to deliver them out -

For this do I now come unto thee - I have sent one out of the place wherein I am that ye may have Light - I have given unto him the power and the authority to give unto thee all that is necessary unto thee -

I say he is now prepared for his part - When ye have received him and of him great shall be thy work and ye shall be blest - Ye shall be blest and ye shall know that which ye are to do - So be it such as ye have waited for -

I am now prepared for my part - Now ye shall be prepared for that which ye are to do -

Let it be recorded that ye shall be prepared that ye might give unto them that which shall be unto them their salvation - I say ye shall be as my hand and as my mouth made manifest unto them -

And too I say I have other hands and other mouths -

I say I shall cause them to be raised up - and prepared for this part for there is much to be done - And I have said that there is little time before I shall come into the world in physical form - even as I have come unto thee - I say even as I have come unto thee -

I say too - Even as my brother and Christed Sananda has come unto thee that ye may have this part - for ye have asked that ye might be lifted up - Ye have given of thyself that this might be accomplished -

Bless them which do come and are lifted up -

Blest shall they be -

Blest am I that I might come unto thee - for do I not know thee and remember thee before ye went out into darkness wherein ye forgot me So be it ye shall return and I am glad -

So be it and Selah -

I am Sanat Kumara

Sister Thedra of the Emerald Cross

Sanat Kumara speaking unto thee -

Blessings on thee my children which have come unto this altar - In the name of the Most High Living God shall ye be blest - I say unto thee ye shall be blest of Him for He has sent me that He might be glorified in the world of men through thee - I say I come in His name unto thee that He, the Father might be glorified in the earth through thee - Such is my work -

I say ye shall receive thy new part and thy part shall be a glorious one indeed - Blest shall ye be - I am with thee that ye may begin thy new work - And I say one shall come unto thee which shall give unto thee great light and cause thee to have comprehension - So be it and Selah - Blest are they which are given comprehension -

Be ye as one which have my hand upon thee and I shall bless thee by day and by night - So be it and Selah -

When ye have given unto them that which has been recorded for them ye shall begin a new part for them and it is begun now - I say it has now begun - And it is to be as none other has been - for it is to be given unto the ones which have prepared themselves to receive it - and for this have ye been prepared -

Now with this date - shall ye set aside the ones which have been unto themself true and the ones which have asked for words from this altar and unto them shall ye give the following parts - And these parts shall be called the "Portions of the Sibors" - Yet they shall be the ones which are kept for the ones which have followed the first ones - And NONE OTHER shall receive these - I say NONE OTHER shall receive these after this date -

Blest are they which follow the way set for them -

I am so minded to bring them out of bondage -

I am with thee unto the end - I am Sanat Kumara -

Sister Thedra of the Emerald Cross

Sanat Kumara speaking -

Beloved of my being - I am come unto thee this morning that ye may be blest of my presence - I say unto thee - Sing praises of joy from the depth of thy being - Sing! Let it ring forth from the depth of thy being -

So be it I shall sing from the center of my being that ye may be filled to overflowing and I say thy cup shall be filled - Let it!

So be it that I am one with thee and ever shall be - I am now come that ye may be given a new part - So have ye accepted it in the name of the Most High Living God - And I am glad - For I say great shall be thy joy -

I am now at thy service - Command of me that which ye will and I shall bring it to pass - Amen and Selah -

Blest are they which serve the Light - And I say great shall be their reward - for I have seen it and it is for the ones which have been unto themself true and returned unto their Source of Being - And they shall see God face to face - Amen and Selah -

Blest are they which are true unto themself - and which do return this day -

Alas! Not all are true - I am sad for this - Yet I am not as one fainting for I say unto thee I am not of them and they are not of me - They have gone the way of flesh - I have gone the way of Light and I am prepared to bring them out when they ask of the Light and when they turn their face homeward - I shall then rush unto their side that they may receive their inheritance - Even as I have received mine -

I say that when they turn unto the Source of their Being I shall give of myself that they may receive of me as I have received of Him the Father - Such is my part -

Amen and Selah -

Now I bless him which has returned unto this altar -

Blessed shall he be and blest is he - I say blest shall he be -

Blest is the work of his hand - Amen - So be it - And so shall it be.

Amen and Amen -

I am with thee and I am glad -

I am thy brother - Sanat Kumara

Sister Thedra of the Emerald Cross

Sanat Kumara speaking -

Beloved of my being - Blest are they which gather themself together in the name of the Father Son and Holy Ghost - Amen and Selah -

I am speaking unto thee now as an elder brother and I say ye which have come unto this altar shall be as one on whose shoulders rests great responsibility - And this is given unto thee as part of thy own preparation - for ye shall not shirk thy responsibility - For it is given unto every man to be his own porter and his own <u>path</u> for he shall be the path - And I say he shall walk which way he wills - for none shall be unto him his carter -

He shall bring himself into the place wherein I am - I say he shall write his own passport - He shall come of his own free will -

Too I say - When ye have fully said with thy whole heart and thy whole self - (Ye have been given this many times yet ye have as yet not said this with all thy strength) "Father - Thy will be done in me - by me through me - and for me" - ye shall be as one permitted to pass the gate For none shall be kept out which is thus prepared - And for this have we waited -

Now I have said I speak unto thee as an older brother - It is so and be ye as one so minded to hear me - And I shall say unto thee that which shall profit thee - Ye have given little thought unto that which I have said and ye have passed it over lightly - And ye have not heard me - nor have ye felt my fingers touch thine -

I say I have reached out unto thee and ye have not lifted up thy face nor reached thy hand that I might touch thee - Ye have not as yet felt my presence - Nor have ye asked for me -

Go into thy own secret place and ask for revelation and I shall come in and sup with thee and ye shall council with me and I shall give unto thee a part separate from all others - So be it and Selah -

I am thy Sibor and thy older brother - Sanat Kumara

Sister Thedra of the Emerald Cross

Sanat Kumara speaking -

Blest art thou and blest are they which come unto this altar for the purpose of learning of the greater things -

Now I say unto thee - Ye shall give these Scripts unto none which have not been thru the first of the Portions of the Sibors - for therein is wisdom - I say they shall be as ones which have a mind to comprehend these things which I say unto thee -

They shall now be as ones which discipline themself for that part which shall be given unto them to do - And there shall be much to do - And all which are prepared for the work shall be as ones obedient unto the law of the temple and the Masters therein -

I say they shall be true unto themself and be as ones which can discipline themself and with this shall end the reading of the temple work until they have finished the Portions - which was given in the School of the Seven Rays -

So be it that they shall be at all times at liberty to ask for any counseling at this table - And they shall not be denied -

Blest are they which do ask - for it is now come when great shall be thy duties within this place - And it is given unto me to know what is to be done - I say ye shall be as one prepared for thy new part and ye have earned this part for thy own -

Ye have been true unto thyself and ye have obeyed all commands and ye have hastened to obey them - So be it the better part of wisdom.

Ye shall say unto them as I would say that they are not as yet prepared to receive me - And when they are I shall come unto them and sibor them - And sibor them in ways of the wise - So be it and Selah -

I am with thee and I AM -

I AM - Forever and forever

One with my Source of Being -

And I know myself to Be -

So be it and Selah -

Sanat Kumara

Sister Thedra of the Emerald Cross

Sanat Kumara speaking -

Blest art thou and blest are they which come unto this altar in the name of the Most High Living God - So be it and Selah -

Be ye as ones which hear me in this - for ye shall be as ones mindful of thy own divinity and of thy own part which have been given unto thee - And ye shall now discipline thyself for that which shall be done.

I say that ye shall be given a part and it is necessary that ye discipline thyself for it - And ye shall bring thy whole self unto this altar as a living sacrifice - And I say unto thee - Ye shall be as one which has thy <u>own</u> fortune within thy own hand - for no man shall have the power to deprive thee of it - And no man shall add to it -

I say ye have found favor with them which do gossip and which do prattle - And ye have now turned from them - Yet ye shall be reminded of thy own prattling and of thy own idle words -

I say ye shall be as ones mindful of thy words - for they are powerful weapons and they are things which work either for weal or woe - Be ye mindful of every word which goes out of thy mouth - for ye shall come to know the wisdom thereof -

I say ye shall be as one prepared for a new part - Yet until ye learn the wisdom of silence ye shall wait -- Such is my word unto thee -

Blest am I that I have been allowed to come unto thee for this part. So be it and Selah -

I am Sanat Kumara

Sister Thedra of the Emerald Cross

Sanat Kumara speaking -

Beloved of my being - I am now come that they shall have the greater part - And for this have they waited -

Blest are they which do receive the greater part -

I am now prepared to bring them into the place wherein I am - When they have given unto themself the proper attention - and when they have properly prepared themselves -

Yet they have not given unto me credit for being that which I am - I say I am not afar off - Nor am I a dream - I am not a myth nor am I a legend - And I am for the first time within this place prepared to open up the door that they may pass - And I say none other shall pass - for it is not the better part of wisdom -

Bless them and give unto them that which shall prepare them - I say they shall be as ones prepared for any emergency - for there shall be emergencies and there shall be catastrophes - And there shall be sorrow. So be it they shall be as ones on whose shoulders rests great responsibility -

Go forth and say unto them these things and I shall give unto thee the power and the strength to give them that which shall prepare them for this part -

Now ye may share this with them which has gathered here - And too I say they shall study their parts - and prepare themself to receive these Sibors which shall be unto them great light -

I am not of a mind to give unto babes my pearls without price -

So be it I am prepared to give unto them - As they are prepared to receive - And NO MORE!

My mission is to unto them as I have received and no more can I do.

Bless them and give unto them as ye have received - Be ye blest of me and by me -

I am thy Sibor and thy brother - Sanat Kumara

Sister Thedra of the Emerald Cross

Sanat Kumara speaking -

Blest are they which walk which way their fortune bids - without complaint -

I say thy fortune has been prepared through the eons of time and it is now a time of garnering in - A time of reaping - And the reaping shall bring both joy and sorrow -

And I say that sorrow there shall be - And it shall behoove thee to prepare thyself with great strength of character and with the greatness which is fortuned unto the initiate -

I say ye shall be fortuned great sorrow - And great shall be thy torment be rebellious of that which ye have fortuned unto thyself -

Ye shall be as one which has prepared thyself in humility and thanksgiving for I say unto thee ye shall be as one which has taken embodiment at this time that ye might clean up that which ye have dunged - I say ye have dunged within thy own places of abode -

Ye have destroyed that which would now be unto thee great comfort - Ye have gone the long way to close out that which ye care not to remember -

I say bring all thy sins out from their hiding place and lay them on the altar of the Most High Living God - And forgive thyself all thy transgressions of the law - And ye shall be as one forgiven - for the Father has forgiven thee lean thou hast sinned - So be it that ye have to clean thy so called house of all the pettiness - all thy offenses against the law and against thy own self and ye shall find thy own way - Such is the law -

Blest are they which know the law and abide by it - And pity is he which knows it and transgresses it -

Be ye as one mindful of thy own divinity - And walk accordingly - Be ye as ones prepared for the greater part -

I am, and I know I AM one with the Father-Mother God -

So be it I am thy brother and thy Sibor - Sanat Kumara

Sister Thedra of the Emerald Cross

Sanat Kumara speaking -

With my hand upon thee this day shall I lead thee - I shall bless thee and I shall give unto thee that which ye may give unto them - for this day do I give unto thee a new dispensation whereby ye may come into the place wherein I am and whereby ye may have thy inheritance in full.

For it is now come when ye shall be prepared for the greater part and ye shall prepare thyself to receive it in the name of the Most High Living God - And when this is accomplished ye shall then receive the assistance of all the Sibors and any council which so ever deems fit to assist thee in thy ascent -

Be ye blest of all them which do sit in council - for thy preparation and they are many - Blest are they for they know that they are one with the Father and they know the law and abide by it - I say blest are all which do abide by it - for they shall be greatly rewarded -

They shall see God face to face - Amen - Hallelujah - and Hallelujah - Forever shall I praise the Father which has sent me forth that this day may be brought into manifestation -

I am one with Him and I AM he which has been and is called the Ancient of Days - I am one of the Keepers of the Flame - I am he which is and which was the guardian of the flame - I give unto thee this day a new law and a new dispensation - And I say unto thee: ye are no longer under the old law - nor are ye of the old order - Ye have been given a new dispensation whereby ye may come the safer route -

I say this day ye may drink of the water of life it and when ye so choose to prepare thyself for such as the Father has willed unto thee - Blest are they for I say all which drink of the liquid substance of life shall not taste of death - for they shall be as one which shall be reborn of God the Father - For all which drink of the substance of life shall pass from the old body into his new body as one made new - As one made perfect - And he shall ascend unto God the Father even as them which have gone the Royal Road -

Blest are they for they shall not pass thru this gate again -

I am - And I know myself to Be - So be it and Selah -

I am Sanat Kumara -

Sister Thedra of the Emerald Cross

Sanat Kumara speaking -

Now it is come when ye shall see me face to face and I am glad - I say ye shall now see me face to face - And for this shall ye be prepared and yet shall be glad for thy preparation - For I say unto thee: ye are as ones which shall be unto the world great light - Ye know not the part which ye are now given - Ye are as ones playing thy part upon a darkened stage - Neither do ye know that ye are the director of thy part.

I have said unto thee "Ye write thy own passport into the place of my abode" - It is so and so be it - for it is the law that ye prepare thyself for thy parts which ye play - that which is given unto thee to do -

And now it is come when ye shall be called out of thy bed at the midnight hour and ye shall answer that call - And ye shall be as ones which have prepared thyself in silence - Ye boast not of thy accomplishments - Nor of thy greatness - Nor of thy wisdom - Ye walk as the initiate - Ye go in and out among them as one of them - Yet ye give not the bitter cup - Nor do ye take part in their frivolity -

Ye give no offense or take no offense - Ye look unto no man for thy salvation - And ye give unto the Father Credit for thy Being - And unto thy benefactors Credit for thy WELL Being - And ye give unto no man that which is given unto thee for thy own strength and for thy own preparation -

Now I say unto thee my child Thedra - this shall be read unto them at this time and they shall remember these my words and take heed of them - I say that they shall heed them well -

And I am mindful of that which is said and done and I go not out of my place that I might hear - I am mindful of my oneness with God the Father - and I know myself to be - Therefore I go not neither do I come, I AM -

And I say when they have prepared themselves I shall appear unto them and they shall see me and council with me - For this have they waited - I say I am not a fool - And I am not easily deceived -

I say that which is wise and prudent - So be it I have spoken wisely and with love - And I am near unto thee and ye shall be blest of me and by me - So be it and Selah -

I am Sanat Kurara

Sister Thedra of the Emerald Cross

Sarah - Mother of Abraham speaking -

My Beloved - From out the fullness of time have I revealed myself unto thee and for this am I now come that ye may be blest of Me - even as others are blest -

The ones which have returned unto Me pure even as they went out from Me - I say the ones which have returned unto Me shall go out from Me no more - They shall abide within the Light forever - And I am glad For it is long that I have awaited this day when these which now are prepared shall be brought in -

I say for this day have I waited - I am glad that they are prepared and as the grain from the fields shall be garnered in -and for this have I sent out ones from My place of abode for this part -

I am forever ready to receive them and it is My part to receive them and to give unto them of Myself that they may abide within My place of abode forever - Yet I say they shall be free to go and come even as I am free -

For I say unto thee - They shall be masters of all things - They shall be as one with the Father and they shall be Co-Creator with Him in Love-Wisdom - and Harmony - This is Law - I say this is Law And too I speak unto thee as the law - for I am one with it and there is no difference - for there is not anything created <u>wisely</u> which is separate from Me -

And that which is brought forth into manifestation is thru and by the law - Yet the ones in darkness know it not -

They misuse it and they create unwisely - and for this are they tormented - I say they MISUSE the energy which is portioned out unto them - And they shall be as ones to blame for all their torment and for all their woes -

Pity are they which have within their hand the power of the law and misuse it for their own satisfaction - So be it they shall reap the consequences thereof - This is a law no man escapes -

Blest is he which comes unto Me of his own free will - I am thy Mother from which ye have gone out and to which ye shall return -

So be it and be it so -

Sarah Mother of Abraham has spoken well

Sister Thedra of the Emerald Cross

Sananda Speaking -

Blest of My being - Be ye blest of Me and by My Presence for this day do I come unto thee as One sent unto thee of God the Father - for the purpose of delivering thee out of bondage - And I say ye shall be as ones free to choose thy way -

Yet I say unto thee which has chosen this path that I have come unto thee for the purpose of giving unto thee as I have received of the Father God even as He has willed unto thee - I say He has given unto Me My Inheritance in full - So be is that ye shall be given as ye are prepared to receive -

Now hear Me and remember My Words - Mark them well - for I shall let them go forth from Me but once - and ye shall profit by them And I say unto thee - Be ye as wise as the serpent and as silent as the Sphinx - for this is the day for which ye have waited -

And I say ye give not thy pearls unto babes which know not their worth - And for this have they been pilfered and My servants rendered up unto Pilate - I say they give the pearls which are meant for THEM unto the foolish - which do rend them asunder -

Now I say when ye have learned this lesson well - I shall give unto thee in abundance -

I shall make thee guardian of Great Treasure - I shall give unto thee the Keys unto the Kingdom -

I am guardian of the keys and I guard them well - Yet ye shall be trained in the ways of Wisdom and Silence - for none pilfer My store house - I say none come without passport - for I give not of My store unto the unjust and the profane - I say I give not of My store unto the profane and the unjust - Blest are they which do come via the gate. I am He which is the guardian and I am He which awaits thy coming.

I am He which is known as Jesus the Christ in the Earth and which is and has been known in this Temple as - Sananda - Son of God -

So I am - and I AM - So be it and Selah -

Sister Thedra of the Emerald Cross

Sarah - Mother of Abraham speaking unto thee My Child - This is a part separate and apart from the other Temple messages which has been given unto thee - I say ye shall say unto them that I am their Eternal Mother - I AM and because I AM - they are - I say they are - because I AM - Now were this not so ye should not BE -

For this do I now speak unto thee that this day bring forth fruit of a new kind and I say it shall -

For I shall lift them which have the will to return unto Me - And I shall make of them that which has been given unto them of the Father-Mother when they were sent out from Us - as part of Us - I say that when they were sent out that they were as the Spoken Word made manifest - and perfect in all ways - And there is the wisdom of creating in Our Image -

I say We create perfect - And too I say that in the world of darkness they have forgotten Us - They have turned from Us - And they have thought themself wise - And they have created like unto the whore - Imperfect have they created - in a fashion which has tormented them - Now they are sick unto death! And they call for help

When they call out for wisdom many shall be sent unto them - and they shall be of a mind to learn and they shall be given comprehension. And they shall be blest of the Father for He shall give unto them the power and the authority to create like unto Him - And therein is wisdom. So be it and Selah -

Let this be recorded - That there are none so foolish as the ones which thinks himself wise - And none so sad as he which betrays himself or his trust -

Blest are they which are true unto themself and return unto Me this day - For I shall give unto them that which I have kept for them - I shall give unto them the power and the authority to say that which I would say - They shall speak the words I put into their mouth - They shall do that which I would do - They shall sing the Songs of Sarah - They shall be as ones which have the mind which is in Me - and they shall error not -

Blest shall they be for they shall walk with Me and talk with Me - And they shall know as I know -

Praise thy Father God which has sent thee out - Sing unto Him praise of Joy and Gladness - Forever and Forever -

I have spoken unto thee from out the Inner Temple wherein all things are known -

So be it and Selah - I am thy Mother

Sister Thedra of the Emerald Cross

Soretus Speaking -

Beloved of My being - I come unto thee this day that they may receive Me - I say by thy hand shall be recorded these My Words - And for this have ye been prepared -

I say ye have prepared thyself that ye night receive Me - And for this do I come unto thee this day - So shall I bless thee with My

Presence and I shall bless them which come unto this altar in the name of the Father Son and Holy Ghost - So be it and Selah -

I say I am now prepared to give unto each a part for which they have prepared themself - And so be it that none shall have the same, part for no part shall be like unto the other - I say no two parts shall be the same - And none shall quibble over his part - for I say all parts are of importance in this Plan which is unfolding before thee -

Now ye shall say unto them in the name of the Most High Living God that they shall give unto the Father all the Credit - all the Glory - and give thanks in all things - And I say unto them they shall see the wisdom thereof -

Blest are they which have the comprehension of such as I say unto thee and blest shall they be - Be ye blest by Me and of Me - for receiving Me into the place of thy abode - for I come unto thee from afar - For this day I come as one for the first time - I say I come unto thee through the Mighty Council of Sun Spa - wherein is the Mighty Council which has for Its Head - the Father of Us All - Which has given unto Us Being.

I say We give unto the Source of Our Being all the glory and all the praise - And from this Council do I say that which I am permitted by law - I say that shall bring unto thee much Light - for this is thy preparation unto the Greater Revelation -

Now was it not said - This is the day of preparation? So be it and it is so!

Now for the first time in the history of man I speak unto the child of Earth - And I say I come through the Council of Sun Spa that ye may have this revelation - And for this have ye prepared thyself - And ye shall give unto them which is wise and prudent -

I rest within the place of My abode and I shall speak with thee again.

I bless them with the fullness of My Being - And I am glad - Bless thee O My Soul - I am thy Brother of the Council of Sun Spa

Sister Thedra of the Emerald Cross

"The Door is Opened Wide"

"Holy Communion"

Sarah, Mother of Abraham speaking unto thee -

Harken unto Me, Oh My children - From out My Being I speak unto thee for the purpose of bringing thee home.

For the first time have I said this unto thee - I come that ye may know Me, even as I know thee, and ye have walked in thy sleep with great longing and torment.

Now "the door has been opened wide" and I have prepared a Blessed One that she may enter in and commune with Me and give unto thee as she has received of Me.

Be ye blest for this is a new day and the sun doeth shine on the eastern horizon and soon ye shall awaken. Then ye shall receive thy inheritance in full and ye shall walk with assurance and ye shall go and come freely and ye shall have no limitations and ye shall be as one with thy God the Father - Ye shall know thyself to be a Son of the Most High Living God.

Blest are they which have this comprehension.

Be ye as ones which have prepared thyself for this communion for ye shall come to know the meaning of <u>Holy Communion</u> and ye shall give unto no man credit for giving unto thee nor taking from thee the right to receive it.

It shall be in no wise given unto any man to judge thy fitness, or thy unfitness to receive Holy Communion. It is fortuned unto me to be thy Eternal Mother which has given unto thee expression through the law of divinity, and I am not the judge, I judge not, I Am the Mother and the Mother has not taken the seat of judgement - She is the feminine part of thy Father God, and He is not divided.

Yet He Is and I Am - Yet we are one and as One We bring forth by the law of love, peace and harmony. Each and every spoken word which creates perfect We send forth no word of discord. No particle of matter do we bring into imperfection - NOT that there is no imperfection.

I say ye have followed the dragon - he which has been cast down, and ye have followed him knowing not - He is the traitor of traitors! And I, even his Eternal Mother, await his return.

Yet I say he shall redeem his works; He shall be as one cast down until he has redeemed all his handiwork - He shall be as one banished until he has brought out of bondage all that he has bound.

I say he has bound them which he now holds fast.

Yet let this go on record that not even he which is known as Lucifer can hold thee against thy own free will. I say thy own free will is thy shield and thy buckler

I say when ye so will to return unto Me - I shall send a legion to thee that ye may be unbound.

I say none shall bind thee against thy will. So be it that one of My Sons shall be sent unto them and they shall know Him, for I say the day of thy blindness shall end. And too, I say the Anti-Christ shall be as naught! For long have they reigned

I say their day is passed - Yet ye shall see many manifestations which shall disturb thee and ye shall be filled with doubts and fears.

Say not that they have power over thee - and give unto them NO CREDIT!

I shall give unto thee the power to defeat them, I say ye shall hold fast unto My hand and ye shall call out unto the Host of Light and ye shall be heard and answered. Blest are they which ask for Light.

I have spoken unto thee wisely - So be it I shall touch thee and ye shall be quickened and ye shall know, and know that ye know.

I Am thy Eternal Mother - Known as Mother Sarah -

Recorded by Sister Thedra of the Emerald Cross

"The Sacrifice"

Sarah - Mother of Abraham speaking -

O, My Children - Blest art thou this day, blest shall ye be - for it is now come that ye shall go into the place which has been prepared for thee.

I say one has gone before thee to prepare a place for thee.

It is finished and it is accomplished that one has set up an altar within that place which has for its foundation a square of six cubits - whereupon thy own names are written.

I say ye have been chosen for this part, for thru the times and half time ye have been upon the altar.

I say ye have been Priest and Priestess, ye have given thy physical form for thy Brothers - ye have lain aside thy garment of flesh that they might have Light.

Ye have guarded the records with thy physical strength, for <u>which ye have sacrificed thy physical body</u> - ye have gone out into the wilderness for the sake of protecting the Faith - Ye have gone out from Atlantis with the records - ye have been unto thy trust true in time past.

Now I say unto thee O My Sons and My Daughters: Be ye not turned aside at this hour, for it is near time when great sorrow shall come upon thee and ye shall prepare thyself this day, for it is so close upon thee, yet I see thee floundering and waving to and fro as a twig which bloweth as by a wind. While it is time I ask of thee turn from thy little way, thy puny way, the way which ye will and ye shall be led into the place wherein thy name is written - I say unto thee - Falter not!

For great shall be thy reward - blest are they which do come in this day - be ye blest of Me and by me - I am thy Eternal Mother Sarah -

Recorded by Sister Thedra of the Emerald Cross

Why We Are Here

The Way of the Initiate"

I, Sanat Kumara speaketh unto thee from the place wherein I Am as one alert and as one prepared.

I say I have given of Myself that this day may bring forth the ones which shall carry the banner of the Christ Light.

I say they shall be raised up in this day and they shall be as ones which have come into embodiment for this purpose. I say that they which have prepared themself for this age are within embodiment for the purpose of bringing about their own redemption, and as they gain their own freedom they shall in turn give unto their fellow man a helping hand.

I say they which shall find their eternal freedom this day shall be unto others which are yet in darkness Sibor.

They which go the Royal Road shall reach out unto the brother which is to follow and give unto him a hand - and he shall be as one which has passed the great initiation and he shall be as one free from all bonds, all bondage, He shall be as one unbound. He shall have his leg-irons removed and he shall find his eternal freedom.

He shall be released from the wheel of rebirth, he shall no longer be subject unto the law of gravity, nor shall he be subject unto the law of gravitation. He shall know the law governing his Being. He shall be as one free to go and come unto any galaxy; he shall conquer all things and shall master all things.

There shall be no mystery for he shall know the law and he shall command the elements and they shall obey in love and in wisdom. He shall be one with God the Father and he shall know himself to be and he shall give unto Him, God the Father, all the credit and unto Him all the glory forever and forever.

So be it the way of the initiate - Amen and Selah and Amen.

Blest art thou and blest shall ye be.

I am Sanat Kumara -

Recorded by Sister Thedra of the Emerald Cross

Thy Father/Mother Has Called Thee Home

Sarah speaking -

O, My children - Have I not gathered thee in - Have I not brought thee together. Have I not spoken unto thee for the purpose of awakening thee. Have I not been unto thee comfort in the hours of thy unknowing. Have I not spoken unto thee in the hours of thy sleep?

Have ye not remembered Me unknowingly? Have ye not remembered Me in the days of thy longing - Have ye not longed to return unto Me in the hours of thy search. Have ye not asked that ye may return unto the place from which ye went out - have ye not wandered far afield since ye went from Me?

Now hear Me, O my children, and be ye as one which has My hand upon thee - For I shall touch thee and ye shall remember Me.

For the first time I say unto thee - <u>Thy Father/Mother has called thee home in this day</u> - So shall ye arise! And come of thy own free will I say none shall bring thee against thy own free will. Blest are they which come of their own free will blest are they which come of their own accord. I say when ye are so minded ye shall be as one prepared - for there shall be a legion sent for to prepare thee.

Yet ye shall do thy part, and then they shall do theirs, and this is the law.

Blest are they which come unto thee for the purpose of bringing thee in. I Am within the place of my abode prepared to receive thee, and glad shall they be which come. I say all which do come shall be glad for all their preparation.

I say ye shall give thanks for all thy suffering, all thy torment, and ye shall add naught unto another's bitter cup. Ye shall not give unto another pain, nor inflict upon him anything whatsoever which shall add unto his burden, nor shall ye deprive him of his lessons, for it is but his preparation. So be it and Selah.

I am with thee unto the end - I am thy Mother Eternal

Recorded by Sister Thedra of the Emerald Cross

Sanat Kumara

Beloved of My Being, be ye this day prepared for that which shall be done. There shall come unto thee one which shall bring unto thee a plan. And it shall be of a sort which is in keeping with the law - and ye shall go into the place wherein ye shall go and therein ye shall talk with the one which is prepared to give unto thee assistance, and ye shall prepare a plan whereby ye shall be given such assistance necessary for this work.

I say these two shall be of assistance in this plan, and it is fortuned unto Me to know, for I have brought them forth that they may be brought together and they shall be as ones which have My hand upon them.

Now I say unto thee, give not unto them power over thee - look unto them for nothing, and ye shall be blest of Me and by Me.

Be ye as one which has My hand upon thee and ye shall be led in all thy ways. So be it and Selah.

I am thy Sibor - Sanat Kumara.

Sara, Mother of Abraham is My Eternal Mother, from which I have gone out - I give unto Her my gratitude, My thanks and praise for giving unto Me being.

I bless the ones which ask of the Father/Mother God - I speak in their name. I command and it is done, by the authority which has been invested within Me. I give unto them the glory for My Being. I know Myself to be one with them for I am now within the place wherein there is no mystery, no darkness, and for this have I come unto thee that ye too might receive thy inheritance in full. That ye may return unto the place of thy going out.

Now it is come when ye shall come out from among them and be fortuned that which the Father has willed unto thee. If ye so choose ye may come into the place wherein I am, and ye shall be delivered from all bonds forever. Yet none shall bring thee against thy own free will.

I say ye shall choose for thyself thy own path. Yet I say unto thee blest are they which choose wisely. So be it and Selah.

I have spoken unto thee many times and ye are yet within the sleepers realm. I say ye shall arise and return unto the place from whence ye went out, wherein ye shall have thy eternal freedom. I am with thee and I shall be unto the end.

Sanat Kumara

Recorded by Sister Thedra of the Emerald Cross

"Engraved upon Solid Gold Leaves -

They Shall Bear Witness"

Blest Am I, and blest shall ye be, for I am privileged to come unto thee that I might speak unto thee thusly. I say unto thee in the name of the most High Living God that it is now come when ye shall be as one prepared for the greater part, and ye shall come into the place wherein I am as one prepared, and ye shall stand before the altar of white alabaster, whereupon ye shall find the words written by thy own hand upon the day when ye stood upon Holy ground for the first time in this age. I say ye shall again within this day stand before the <u>great white altar</u>.

And ye shall read that which was written by thy own hand, which is engraved upon solid gold leaves, whereupon ye shall find thy name, thy number and thy symbol.

I say before this altar ye shall be unveiled, and I say ye shall stand as one free, for in that place wherein ye shall go ye shall find thy beloved Brother and Sibor known as Sananda, Son of God, and herein He shall bless thee and give unto thee the gifts which He has kept for thee, and for these have ye waited.

Blest are they which stand within this place - for they shall see Me face to face and I shall give unto them as I have received of God the Father.

Blest are they which come for they shall be even as I am and they shall rejoice forever, for they shall know God the Father even as I know Him, and it shall be cause for rejoicing.

I say unto thee My hand made manifest, ye shall go into all the lands of the Earth as one prepared for that which shall be given unto thee to do. And ye shall be as one on whose shoulders rests great responsibility, and ye shall be as one in authority, for I shall command for thee thy freedom from all bondage forever. So be it and Selah, I have spoken. So let it be and So be it.

Now ye shall give unto them this my word unto thee, and they shall bear witness of that which I have said unto thee and they shall remember that which I have said, for they shall have cause for remembering that which I have said. So be it a time of rejoicing - Amen and Selah.

I am Sanat Kumara

Recorded by Sister Thedra of the Emerald Cross

The Temple of the Great White Mountain

"Altar of White Alabaster"

Blessed of my being - Blest art thou and blest shall ye be.

Ye shall now say unto them that which I shall give unto thee to say, and ye shall be as one blest of Me and by Me, for I am now prepared to receive thee into the place wherein stands the Great White Altar of Alabaster.

I say I am now come into the Temple of the Great White Mountain wherein stands the Altar of White Alabaster.

I say ye shall come into this Temple wherein He now sit council for the good of all mankind.

I say that when ye come into this place ye shall stand in awe of its beauty, for therein is a place where no human foot has set... and within this place ye shall find the words which were written upon that 'holy ground' in July - lying upon the altar - I say upon the altar lies the words which was written by the hand at the 'gathering in' in July when ye answered the call.

I say that those words are engraved upon solid gold leaves which are imperishable and ye shall marvel at their beauty. I say ye shall stand in awe of and with the beauty therein,

Blest are they which stand before this altar, for they shall be lifted up. So be it and be it so - Selah.

Be ye as one mindful of Us and We shall draw nigh unto thee, and ye shall be glad. Bless them which sit with thee and say unto them as I would say that they shall come to know Me as I know them and they shall be glad.

Praise His Holy Name and rejoice forever. So shall ye be blest - I am with thee and I shall bless thee by day and by night.

I am thy Sibor and thy brother Sananda

Recorded by Sister Thedra of the Emerald Cross

SANANDA

Beloved of My Being - I call thee from thy bed at this hour for the purpose of giving unto thee a plan - And within this plan is no error - And within this is wisdom -

Now be ye blest of Me and by My presence - for I come that ye may be blest - and for this do I speak unto thee at this hour.

Now be ye as one prepared for the next part - for there is much to be done and ye shall go into the southland wherein ye shall find one which has a part within this temple and within this temple shall he work.

He shall be as one alert and prepared for this part and he shall go unto all ends to give unto the plan his undivided efforts and his strength He shall be unto thee thy hand and thy foot - He shall give unto thee that which is necessary for that which is to be done - He shall be as one which has the qualification of a SOLDIER OF FORTUNE - He shall wear upon his brow the wrinkles of time - He shall be aware of thy needs - He shall bring thee into the place wherein there is one other which has counseled with him on thy behalf and he shall be as one with thee and he shall give unto thee great comfort - for this is his part - For this has he been prepared -

I say he has been prepared for this part and ye shall now go into the place wherein he is and ye shall be as one on whose shoulders rest the responsibility of this contact - I say ye shall now prepare thyself for this part - for in the days ahead ye shall answer the call - and great shall be thy reward - So be it and Selah.

I am now prepared to give unto thee that which ye need for thy own welfare and that which is essential unto the plan and for the House of Sananda-Sanat Kumara -

I say they which do dwell within the house wherein ye are shall abide by the law set forth and they shall be as ones which give of themself that the plan be accomplished and brought to fulfillment - I say that they shall be obedient at all times unto my Oracle - they shall share the responsibility of the work - that which goes to keep up the temple in which ye abide.

I say that ye shall consider thy dwelling place a temple wherein ye shall work for a time and therein ye shall dwell as Brother and Sister of the Order of Sarah -

Ye shall serve as one at the same altar - Ye shall be unto the other comfort and ye shall not give unto another the bitter cup - Neither shall be ye as one which rides upon the back of the other - I have said that each shall share his responsibility with joy in his heart and he shall go about his duty without being told - Yet when one shirks his responsibility he shall go from the temple as an outcast - with no word of condemnation for his fellows and he shall receive none from them.

I have given unto thee the law of the temple and I say the law shall be obeyed -

I am within the place wherein I am for the purpose of bringing this plan into fulfillment - And I shall not be denied - For I am not about to betray Myself or My trust -

I say I am a task master - And I am not afraid for myself nor am I afraid for My servants - for I am near unto them and I shall give unto them the protection necessary for this work -

I do protect and bless My servants - Know this: I am not alone in this - I have brought with Me a legion of Workers which have received of the Father Their inheritance - even as I have received Mine - So be it that They too are prepared to bring thee out of bondage - and to bless thee and to deliver thee up -

Be ye mindful of Them and they shall draw near unto thee -

I am thy Sibor and thy Brother -

Sananda -

Sister Thedra of the Emerald Cross

SANANDA

Blest art thou My child - Blest are they which come unto this altar for I come unto thee that ye may be blest-

Hear Me O My children - for I am come that ye may be prepared for the greater part - Have I not said this is the place for and of preparation - I have no other weapons - No other vicissitudes - No others to work with than these which are of the mind to be My sheep - My servants - My brothers -

I say unto thee: ye are My sheep - My brothers - Ye shall be My hands made manifest in the world of men - Ye shall go out before Me to prepare the way before Me - Ye shall be mindful of thy part -

And I say ye shall walk as I would - Ye shall be mindful of Me in all thy ways - Ye shall be unto thyself true -

For there is no way into the secret place to the Most High Living God - except through thy own divinity - Be ye aware of it.

Be ye alert at all times of thy oneness with thy Source of Being -

Bless them which ye come into any contact with daily - Know for them that which they know not - Keep unto thyself that which is given unto thee for thy own progress -

Yet ye shall send out upon the Earth the love and the power which has been willed unto thee of God the Father - which shall come back as the homing pigeon - It shall return a thousand times - ten thousand times multiplied - So be it the law that which ye send out returns to bless thee or to curse thee -

I say ye do bless thyself or ye curse thyself - Ye alone shall be thy gate keeper - Close out that which ye do not wish to receive which is sent out by the unknowing ones - Stand guard at thy own gate and let none enter which are not of the Light -

Bless the ones which know not, yet be no part of their unknowing and put not before them a stumbling block -

Ye are the chosen - Walk ye in the way set before thee - Hold high the lamp which I have given unto thee and I say ye shall walk upright as man - As a son of God which has given unto thee Being and ye shall find thy way into the secret place of the Most High Living God - And glad ye shall be - Amen - So be it and be it so -

I am thy Brother - Sananda -

Sister Thedra of the Emerald

SANANDA

Beloved of My being - Blest art thou and blest shall ye be - be ye blest of My presence for I come that ye may receive this part for them and they shall receive it in the name of the Father, Son and Holy Ghost. Amen and Selah -

Beloved one which I call Bea - Be ye as one which has my hand upon thee - Have I not touched thee in the hours of thy sleep - Have I not breathed upon thee that ye may be as one healed of thy weakness Have I not prepared thee for this part and have I not brought thee out from among them?

Now I say unto thee ye shall be as one prepared for a part which is new unto thee and ye shall be glad - for in all thy ways ye shall be reminded of Me and ye shall give unto Me credit for thy well-being - And bless them which keep watch thru the midnite hours for thy sake -

Be ye as one mindful of the Source of thy being by day and by night and ye shall be as one blest -

Be ye as one on whose shoulders rests great responsibility for ye have been chosen for this part - And I say ye shall be blest For another part is prepared for thee and ye shall be as one prepared to receive it - So be it and Selah -

Now bless them which are with thee and ye shall be blest in turn - So be it and Selah -

I am thy Sibor and thy brother - Sananda -

Sister Thedra of the Emerald Cross

MOTHER SARA

Mother of Abraham am I - I AM thou art - and thou art because I AM.- Blest am I and blest art thou -

Be ye blest of Me - And know thyself to be - for I now reveal Myself that ye may know Me and thy oneness with Me -

Be ye as one which has my hand upon thee and ye shall be as Myself, for I am with thee - I AM with <u>them</u> - Yet they know Me not - And I say within this day shall they come to know Me - for I shall reveal Myself to them which have ears to hear and eyes to see - and they shall speak with Me and walk with Me - So be it and Selah -

Before ye were I AM - I was - I shall ever be - I change not - I go not - Neither do I come - I AM - And I speak the word and I bring into being that which I will - And it becomes that which I speak for I give unto it expression - I give it form - I bring about that which is wise and prudent -

I go into the heart of the Earth - I put therein the gold which has the fortune of being unto Her the Earth, the blood the veins of gold shall be no longer destroyed out of her body - for it is as she was embalmed by the dead - They know not that she, My child which I have caused to be brought into manifestation, has been embalmed before her death -

Nay sayeth I unto them - She shall NOT die - For I say she, My Child - the Earth, which has been brought forth for a purpose which they know not - shall fulfill her mission - And for this is she being prepared -

When it is come that they go so far as to abort her - They shall be caught up short and they shall be removed as by the hand of God - For I say unto thee they shall be removed as by the hand of God - For I say unto thee they shall not abort thy planet Earth Nor shall they be as the ones which shall deliver out the PEARLS -

For My Pearls are no part of their fortune - Blessed are My Pearls - for I have fashioned them of Myself - I have created wisely and justly and they shall be returned unto Me as they went out - And for this do I speak unto thee -

FEAR NOT - for I am within My place of abode for the purpose of receiving them and I am glad this day is come - So be it a glad day - Amen and Selah -

I am Sara - Mother of Abraham -

Sister Thedra of the Emerald Cross

SANAT-KUMARA

For the first time I bring unto thee One from out the silence wherein He has been with the Father/Mother God - as One with Them and as They, He has been within that place - forever a part of Them - He has not separated Himself from Them - And it is the first time in the history of man that He speaks unto man of Earth -

And now I bring unto thee this One which is one with Me in this My part of this work - He has volunteered for this part and He has given of Himself that I may be blest as He has been blest - For this am I glad.

Now ye shall receive of Him that which He has for thee and ye shall give it unto them which are of a mind to receive of Him - And they shall be blest -

BORICH am I and I am come unto thee that ye may come to know Me and I am in the place wherein all things are known - And I am prepared to pass from the point of thy beginning and to enter into thy kingdom as man - and become man even as thy brothers which have descended into thy realm that ye may have Light - Ye shall be as one which is blest to know These which have descended as Sons of God -

I am now prepared to join them within the Great and Grand Temple wherein stands the Great White Altar of Alabaster and wherein are thy written words which was written upon Holy ground - and wherein shall stand the Grand Worthy Master and wherein shall stand thy Master Sananda - Beloved Son of God the Father.

I come within the time which is near and I say great shall be the preparations to receive Me - for there shall be great rejoicing throughout all the Cosmos -

Blest are they which are part of this Great Brotherhood - for within it work the Hierarchy - and all the redeemed of the Earth - All the ascended which are responsible for the Earth and Her redemption - So great is the Word that They have within Their mouth the Power to create worlds without end - and I say They are gods within Their own right - And within Their hand They have the Power to create like unto God the Father - And He has endowed unto Them all that He has and all that He is - And I say unto thee: Be ye not fearful - for They shall not betray Themself - for They are true unto Their trust and They are of the Father sent - And They shall be unto thee all the Father would have Them be -

Be ye at the altar at the day to come and I shall speak with thee -

I am thy Brother and thy Sibor from the Inner Temple wherein the Father abides - So be it and Selah -

Borich

Sister Thedra of the Emerald Cross

Sanat Kumara speaking -

Now ye shall receive of the blessed one which has come into the place wherein I am - And I say unto thee that he is as one which has as yet not taken embodiment as man - He is as one which awaits his physical embodiment - He has not descended into flesh as man and he has not been bound by flesh - for he has never been in the realm of human -

In the realm of light which is not bound by form and which is within the realm of the Father God -

I say unto thee ye shall be as one which has the first communication with him within the realm of man - for he has for thee a part which is separate from that of all the others - And for this have ye waited -

Now ye shall receive him and of him in the name of the Most High Living God - Amen and Selah -

Borich speaking -

Beloved of my being - I am come into the place wherein are thy brothers of Light - And I say I am now prepared to take upon myself a body of flesh and bone - And I shall walk the earth even as thy Saints and even as the Royal Assembly has walked upon thy earthly highways and biways -

I say I shall walk among them as man - As one made flesh and bone I say I shall walk with them and they shall know me not -

For it is now come when great and glorious things shall be accomplished and many shall be as the lamb lifted up by the condor -

I say as the condor lifts up the lamb so shall they be lifted up - and glad shall they be - Blest shall they be -

Now for the first time I speak unto thee thusly - I say that ye shall be blest to receive me and of me and I shall come unto thee as one full grown - Not as a child - For I shall be unto myself both parent and son I shall be unto myself a man and a woman - I shall be neither male nor female - I shall be androgynous - And I shall be unto myself all things for I shall be of the Father/Mother God - I shall be one with them and I shall not separate myself from them -

For this do I come unto thee that ye may be prepared to receive me Blest shall ye be - I am called Borich - Which all things come - Blest are they which do receive me and of me -

I am and I know myself -

Sister Thedra of The Emerald Cross

Sanat Kumara speaking -

Beloved of my being - It is well that ye are within this place - For it is come when one shall come from out the inner temple wherein the Father abides - And he shall walk within the streets and upon the mountain and he shall be as one mocked - For he shall be as none other.

And yet others shall try to imitate him and he shall outshine them all - I say he shall outshine them all - So be it and Selah -

Now for the first time I say unto thee - Ye shall walk with this one and ye shall talk with him for he shall be unto thee all that the Father would have him be - I say ye shall be unto him a disciple - And ye shall be unto him that which I have been unto him - for he has gone the long way to bless thee - He has gone out from his place of abode that he might find thee and I say he shall find thee prepared to receive him - And glad shall ye be -

I say ye shall in turn bless others - And for this shall they be prepared -

Now ye shall say unto them in my name that they shall gather themself together and meditate upon that which has been said unto them according unto the law - And they shall put to use that which has been given unto them and they shall present themself as a living sacrifice before the altar -

They shall bring their hearts - their hands and their free will and surrender them up - that the Father's will might be done in them - through them - by them - and for them -

Then they shall see the wisdom of such instruction - It is the short route - I say it is the safe route and it is the new day - the new dispensation is given unto thee -

Ye are under A NEW LAW - Ye are no longer under the old law - for I have come with so many of my brothers that this may be given unto the world of man <u>this day</u> - (age) -

Now ye may go into the secret place wherein they sit in council for the good of all mankind - and therein ye shall hear for thyself that which is said - And ye shall profit thereby - Then ye shall give unto others that which they have prepared themself for to receive - I say ye shall give unto them in wisdom and in prudence - Such is wisdom -

"They shall not pilfer my pearls" - sayeth the Lord - unto the end -

I am Sanat Kumara -

Sister Thedra of the Emerald Cross

Sanat Kumara speaking -

Beloved of my being be ye blest of me and by me -

I come at this time that they may bear witness of me and that which I say unto them -

For it is now come when they shall be as ones come alive - They shall be as ones on whose shoulders rests their own salvation - They shall be as ones prepared for that which shall be given unto them to do and they shall be as ones responsible for every word which proceeds out of their mouth - They shall be responsible for their own actions and for that which they take up on themself

They shall be as ones which have the will to serve the Father God with their whole heart - with all their strength - with all their might -

And I say no sacrifice is too great - for I know that which is in store for them which does endure - So be it that I have seen the reward - Blest are they which do endure -

I say that when they have sufficiently prepared themself I shall come in and counsel them and I shall personally prepare a part for them which shall profit them - Now ye shall say unto them in my name - that there are none so foolish as the one which thinks himself wise - and none so sad as he which betrays himself -

Be ye as my mouth and as my voice - and say again that they have not heard that which I have said unto them -

They have put words into my mouth* -

They have said that which is prompted by the discarnate spirits - they have given credit unto the ones which are yet bound in the Astral, for that which they do and they say they have learned much -

I say that they serve the dragon - They are not of the Light -

I say they are as yet bound in darkness - and they have not as yet passed from darkness into light - They are bound -

I say that pity is the one bound in darkness - I say again they which are used by the ones trapt within the Astral regions are the pawns of the dark forces - They are the unknowing ones -

I say they know not - They are sad - They think themself wise -

They place upon themself great and glorious mantles and they parade before the mass and they call them their subjects. They hold them in bondage and in "SUBJECTION" - They give unto them no peace - no comfort - And they go into the place wherein they hold forth and make laws which are designed to bind them - They give not of themself - They give unto them no release - They bring unto the populace no salvation - Yet they scorn my brothers - My brothers from out the realms of Light which have come for thy own sake - They give of themself that "They" might be brought out of bondage - freed forever. I say they spit on the work of their hand -

They give nothing -

They take all - The credit - the glory - They give the bitter cup unto the servants -

They think themself wise indeed - Yet I see them as ones running hither and yon as ones held fast within the web of the Astral - which is but the dragon cast out -

I say he, the dragon, is the wily one - He has caused them to be deceived - He has gone the long way to bind them - And they shall be <u>UNbound</u> - And they shall no longer be bound against their will - I say WILL it so that ye be released that ye be unbound - and freed forever!

So be it ye are as one freed!

For I say a host shall come unto thy aid - I say one shall be sent - and he shall give unto thee as he has received - And glad shall ye be -

Blest is he which is sent - And blest shall ye be to receive him -

I am thy older brother - Sanat Kumara -

Sister Thedra of the emerald Cross

*They have put their own interpretation on his words -

Mission Statement

Give the truth to the world. Let it be received where it will. Many will read the messages. Some will accept the truth, others will read through curiosity, a few will ridicule. Yet to all is the truth given, and to all remains the power of choice.

The hope of the world in these times is in spiritualizing all forms of activity---promoting understanding through love and service. These must be the watchwords if the world is to come into lasting peace. We are trying to influence a world that is going astray and could cause undreamed of suffering. We are trying to overcome the thought of materialists and to bring a spiritual outlook into the earthly life. We need the help of all on earth who can think in spiritual terms. The great battle to be fought now is between the spiritual and the material, between idealism and carnalism. You can help by spreading the word---we are asking that you help because the battle may be long and the victory far away.

Halls of Light is not allied with any sect, denomination, political entity, organization, neither endorses nor opposes any cause. There are no dues for membership. Halls of Light is self-supporting through its own voluntary contributions. Halls of Light has but one purpose: to help through encouragement and understanding...

To contact the publishers or to obtain copies of our other books, please contact us at email: goldtown11@gmail.com

Sananda's Appearance

Be ye as one which hast heard Mine Voice and responded unto it - for I speak that ye hear, and I say that which is wise and prudent.

Let it be known that 1, the Lord thy God hast spoken and bear ye witness of Me, for I have made manifest Mineself that ye might know Me - and for this wast these manifestations made.

I say that I have made Mineself manifest that ye might see Me with thine mortal eyes; that ye might bear witness of Me. Yet thine companions saw and believed not; neither did they hear, for they were selfish and unprepared - yet, did I deny them?

I say; I came that they which would might see and hear. I went and came again unto Mine own. So be it that I have found; I have given unto the found that they which know not might know; that they might come to know as thou knowest.

Yet, how many hast turned from Me and persecuted thee for Mine Word. It is said, "Woe unto them which persecute Mine servants." is it not the law which they set into motion?

Yea Mine beloved, I say they bring about their own downfall. So be it that I am a compassionate one, and I would that they know what they do. So be it they shall learn well their lessons. So let it be, for this is the mercy of God, the One which hast sent Me.

So be it. I AM The Wayshower, the Lord thy God

I AM Sananda

Authority to Use the Name Sananda

Sori Sori: Mine hand I have placed upon thine head, and I have given unto thee the authority to use Mine name. For I first showed Mineself unto thee with the Word: "Go feed Mine sheep. Give unto them the name Sananda, by which they shall know Me as the Lord thy God - the Son of God sent that ye be made to know Me - the One sent from out the Inner Temple that there be Light in the world of men."

Now it is come when ones which have the will to follow Me shall come to know Me by that name which I commanded thee to give unto the world as Mine "New Name." There are many which shall call upon the name of Jesus, yet they will deny the New Name as they are want to do. While unto thee I give assurance that I am the One sent that there be Light in the world of men. Now let this be understood, that they which deny Mine New Name deny Me by any name. So be it I have appointed thee Mine spokesman; I've given unto thee the power and authority to speak for being that which I AM. And I say unto thee Mine child whom I have called forth and anointed thee with the Holy Spirit, thy name shall be as it is now called, Thedra - that name I spoke unto thee from out the eth, and thou heard Me and accepted that which I gave unto thee; and wherein have I deceived thee? Wherein have i forgotten thee, or left thee alone?

I say unto thee, Mine hand is upon thee and I shall sustain thee and ye shall come to know that which I have kept for thee. So be it that I have kept thy reward, and at no time shall it be dissipated or scattered, for it is intact. So let this Mine Word suffice them which question thee - let them question, and I shall bear witness for thee. For do I not know Mine servants from the traitor? Do I not reward Mine servants according unto their works or merits? I speak that they might know that I am mindful of mine servants, that I am not a poor puny priest who hast forgotten his servants.

I say unto them, Mine servants shall be glorified above the crowned heads of the nations which have set themselves apart, and denied Me Mine part of Mine Word - for they have turned from Me in their conceit and forgetfulness.

Now let this go on record as Mine Word, and I shall give unto them proof, which are of a mind to follow Me. So be it I have spoken and I am not finished; I shall speak again and again, and I shall raise Mine Voice against them which set foot against Mine servants, and they shall be as ones cast out. So let them ask of Me and I shall enlighten them. So be it I know whereof I speak. Be ye as ones blest to accept Me and know Me for that which I AM.

Sananda

About the Late Sister Thedra

Since the later part of the last Century the Kumara wisdom preserved by Aramu Muru has begun to reemerge into the world. This process began with the late Sister Thedra, whom Jesus Christ appeared physically to while on her deathbed and spontaneously healed her of cancer while she was in the Yucatan, where she had gone to accept her fate, and the will of our Lord Jesus Christ.

That is when something miraculous occurred. Jesus spoke to her saying, "My name is Esu Sananda Kumara" and then sent Thedra down to the Monastery of the Seven Rays to learn the Kumara wisdom. After five years, Thedra was told to return to the United States where she founded the Association of Sananda and Sanat Kumara at Mt. Shasta in California.

While heading this organization, Thedra channeled many messages from Sananda and taught the Kumara wisdom until her passing in 1992. While in the Yucatan it is said that while Sister during the 1960s Thedra was in the Yucatan, she was told a secret by her friend George Hunt Williamson, also known as Brother Philip, who authored Secrets of the Andes, and the SECRET PLACES OF THE LION.

Williamson, confided in his long-time friend Sister Thedra that he intentionally scrambled the reincarnational lineages in order to protect this next generation when they the Mayan Solar Priests, who were the direct line descendants of the Kumara according to prophesy were scheduled to reincarnate or return to fulfill their missions upon Earth, one of which was to relocate these ancient sites where the original records of the Amaru were placed for safe keeping.

Sister Thedra, 1900-1992, spent five years at the abbey undergoing intensive spiritual training and initiations. While in South America in the Yucatan, she had an experience which changed her in an instant when as it is told by her that Jesus Christ physically appeared to her and spontaneously cured her of cancer.

He introduced himself to her by his true, name, "Sananda Kumara," thereby revealing his affiliation with the Venusian founders of the Great Solar Brotherhoods. It was by his command that Sister Thedra went to Peru where in here travels she met Williamson.

Sister Thedra eventually left Peru upon telling her experience there was complete. Even before she returned to the States she met with harsh criticism from the church, which she elected to leave. She then traveled to Mt. Shasta in California and founded the Association of Sananda and Sanat Kumara. A.S.S.K.

You ask, Is There A Difference Between Jesus and Sananda? Our Lords name given at birth by his Father Joseph, and his beloved mother Mary was Yeshua, thus being of the house of David and the order of Yoseph, he would be called Yeshua ben Yoseph. The Roman Emperors placed the name of Jesus upon the sir name of Yeshua, after the Emperor Justinian adopted Christianity as the official faith of Rome, and ordered that the sacred books be compiled, upon approval of a specially appointed council, appointed by the Emperor, into a recognizable and uniform work titled The Bible. Prior to this there never was a Bible per se.

There existed until the time of the Emperor's edict, a selection of many Sacred texts, that were employed in the Sacred Teachings. Many of which were copies of what the Greeks had transposed from the original texts in the Libraries of Alexandria, which were originally compiled by Alexander the Great, and were destroyed by Julius Caesar, fearing that they might prove dangerous to the rule of a Caesar, an Earthly God.

In addition, it kept. (he thought) the knowledge of Alexander's Libraries, out of the hands of the Ptolemy's, who were said to be descended from his bloodline. At the time Caesar had no way of knowing the vast portions of the Library that were already in the Americas, in the Great Universities of the Inca, and the Maya. Yeshua spent many years in the East after his ascension. The good Sheppard, upon his appearances to the Apostles after his ascension told his Apostles that he was in fact going to tend to his Father's other sheep; which means, plainly that he was continuing upon his sacred journey. As the ascended one, Yeshua took to himself the name of Sananda, meaning the Christed one, and Sananda was thus embraced forever more by the Great Solar Brotherhood. To many of you this is all new, to others it will be received as a welcome easing of the wall that has so long separated two sides of the same coin, this is being placed into the ethers and the matrix of thought at this time as it is the time of the Awakening, and the Christos is already emerging into the new consciousness, and mother Earth herself. Sister Thedra and the phenomenon of channeling.

Authority to use the name of Sananda was given to Sister Thedra when Jesus~ Sananda appeared to her in the Yucatan, and cured her instantly of the cancer that had taken her body over. Further, he allowed a picture of his countenance to be taken at that time that she might realize the occurrence was more than a dream. Thedra had a large format camera called a 620 and it had bellows on it and founded out. She used this to take the picture of Sananda.

Sanada's Message to her by Sister Thedra. "Sori Sori: Mine hand I have placed upon thine head, and I have given unto thee the authority to use Mine name. Give unto them the name Sananda, by which they shall know Me as the Lord thy God - the Son of God, sent that ye be made to know me, the One sent from out the inner temple that there be Light in the world of men." Now it is come when ones which have the will to follow Me shall come to know Me by that name which I commanded thee to give unto the world as Mine "New name."

There are many that shall call upon the name of Jesus, yet, they will deny the new name as they are want to do. While unto thee I give assurance that I am the One sent that there be Light in the world of men. Now let this be understood, that they that deny Mine New Name deny Me by any name. So be it I have appointed thee Mine spokesman; I've given unto thee the power and authority to speak for being that which I AM. And I say unto thee Mine child whom I have called forth and anointed thee with the Holy Spirit, thy name shall be as it is now called, Thedra - that name I spoke unto thee from out the ethers, and thou heard Me and accepted that which I gave unto thee; and wherein have I deceived thee? Wherein have I forgotten thee, or left thee alone?"

"I say unto thee, Mine hand is upon thee and I shall sustain thee and you shall come to know that which I have kept for thee. So be it that I have kept thy reward, and at no time shall it be dissipated of scattered, for it is intact. So let this Mine Word suffice them which question thee - let them question, and I shall bear witness for thee. For do I not know Mine servants from the traitor? Do I not reward Mine servants according unto their works or merits? I speak that they might know that I am mindful of Mine servants, that I am not a poor puny priest who has forgotten his servants."

"I say unto them, Mine servants shall be glorified above the crowned heads of the nations which have set themselves apart, and denied Me Mine part of Mine word for they have turned from Me in their conceit and forgetfulness." "Now let this go on record as Mine Word, and I shall give unto them proof, which are of a mind to follow Me. So be it as I have spoken and I am not finished; I shall speak again and again, and I shall rise Mine Voice against them which set foot against Mine servants, and they shall be as ones cast out. So let them ask of Me and I shall enlighten them. So be it I know where of I speak. Be ye as ones blest to accept Me and know Me for that which I AM. The Final Messages on Saturday, June 13, 1992, at exactly 10.00 PM, at the age of 92, Sister Thedra made her final transition from the comfort of her own bed. When the time arrived, she simply took one small breath and slipped quietly away, without pomp or fanfare.

She left as she had lived...as a humble servant for the greater good. The messages that follow were given to Sister Thedra shortly before her transition. They are compiled here to give you some idea of the significance of her passing and of the expansion of the work, as she is now free to work unencumbered by the physical limitations and by the pain which has so encumbered her in the past. She has carried on the work here on the Earth plane for the last 50 years because that's where the work was needed...rest assured that her work now in the higher realms will simply be an extension of that work.

www.ingramcontent.com/pod-product-compliance
Lightning Source LLC
LaVergne TN
LVHW051516070426
835507LV00023B/3135